TOUCHING THE UNIVERSE

TOUCHING THE UNIVERSE

My Favorite Twenty Nights Viewing the Sky

STEVEN R. COE

iUniverse, Inc.
Bloomington

Touching the Universe
My Favorite Twenty Nights Viewing the Sky

iUniverse books may be ordered through booksellers or by contacting:

iUniverse
1663 Liberty Drive
Bloomington, IN 47403
www.iuniverse.com
1-800-Authors (1-800-288-4677)

ISBN: 978-1-4620-0247-4 (sc)
ISBN: 978-1-4620-0249-8 (dj)
ISBN: 978-1-4620-0248-1 (ebk)

Printed in the United States of America

iUniverse rev. date: 03/23/2011

DEDICATION

This book is dedicated to all the people I have enjoyed the sky with over the years. From large star parties to a small group of old friends it has all been a source of joy for me.

A group of Saguaro Astronomy Club (SAC) members ready for a great night of observing in Arizona, far from city lights

All the drawings in this book are my work. Some of the wide-field photographs and digital images were taken by me. Many of the astrophotographs of individual objects are by Chris Schur; some are by Paul Lind. Many of the objects in the southern sky were shot by Jim Barclay and me in Australia. I cannot thank them enough for sharing the images within this book.

Steve Coe

CONTENTS

INTRODUCTION

⁓

I Do Love Sunset

This was written far from the lights of Phoenix, Arizona, and near to the lights of the universe.

Every time I go out to observe the night sky I try to show up early enough to spend some time enjoying the beauty of sunset and twilight. The place that the Saguaro Astronomy Club calls the "Antennas Site" is about one hundred miles west of central Phoenix in the southwestern desert of the United States.

From this location the anticipation of the night beginning starts with our star, the Sun, setting over a distant jagged mountain chain. It is much like the effect of Baily's Beads during a solar eclipse. The last-seen chord of the Sun lights up valleys in the distance. So the Sun does not set as a disappearing upside-down crescent Sun but breaks into pieces and then is gone.

Once the Sun is gone from the sky, the western horizon begins a light show that lasts for nearly an hour, as if the Sun did want to give up its position of brightest orb in the sky. First the horizon takes on a bright yellow cast, and that slowly changes to red and purple. Turning to the eastern horizon you can see the "Girdle of Venus," a pink and purple ring on the other side of the sky from the sunset point. This is the shadow of the Earth receding into space.

At the Antennas Site there is a hill and ridgeline that takes up much of the eastern horizon. As the colors of the Earth to the west reflect off this raised ground they take on the colors of the sky. This part of the Arizona desert becomes yellow and then light red and dark blue as night approaches.

On this particular Saturday night the thin crescent Moon is easily the most obvious thing in the sky once the Sun is gone. The crescent shape is bright and beautiful in the clear desert air, and the glowing earthshine casts a fainter light that "fills in" the globe of the Moon. This is the reflection of the light from the Earth bouncing off the Moon and back to your eye.

The crescent Moon

Now the brighter little points of light are starting to appear. Mars is near Castor and Pollux in Gemini, and Saturn is almost straight overhead. In the east Leo has appeared.

As the fainter stars begin to show themselves, the western horizon fades toward much darker blues. Finally the Sun has given up its opportunity to light up the sky and will have to wait until morning to wake up a sleepy world. Now the sky is left to those who appreciate the darkness of night and the beauty it can bring.

The telescope is all set up and ready to gather up light from those distant planets, stars, and galaxies. The fun is just beginning.

Chapter 1: November 10, 1979

 ⸎

Getting Started

The night sky has always interested me. Even as a child those points of light in the sky were a source of fascination. Some of my best memories from childhood are of going fishing with my grandfather, Fred Rainey. "Pop," as I called him, taught me that the constellations would show me which direction we were traveling in. There was a "North Star," and it even had pointer stars to make certain you knew where it was located. There was also a "South Star"; it was called Antares, and it resided within a giant fish hook that also looked like a scorpion. When Antares moved beyond the western horizon, a giant hunter (Pop said he was a fisherman) called Orion rose up in the east to take its place. Pop was my hero; he could use the stars to steer the boat home. That was amazing stuff to a six-year-old boy.

My mother Emogene and me in 1955; notice the binoculars

I learned more stars and constellations when I joined the Boy Scouts and went after an astronomy merit badge. It took a while to get used to the strange names for the stars. Many of them are Arabic in origin, and it took some time to pronounce and use those names correctly. But I managed and eventually got the merit badge.

Me in my scouting years

By this time it was the sixties and the space age had begun. I remember going outside at the time given in the newspaper and watching a Gemini capsule travel overhead. That tiny dot of light contained two men. Truly amazing! Like so many other people, I remember exactly where I was when the first landing on the Moon occurred, watching on my parent's television as those distorted black-and-white images showed humanity traveling out into the solar system for the first time. It was an amazing feat, and I believed that it would change the world for the better. Ah, the naiveté of a teenager.

5

Because my draft board insisted, I joined the navy in 1970. My father was a career naval aviator (I was born in Pensacola, Florida, the largest naval air station in the world), so I knew what I was getting into. Just because I was curious about it, I decided to become a submarine sailor. The good news is that the navy kept their part of the bargain and I got a good education as a nuclear power technician and a chance to see the world. I was stationed in Pearl Harbor, and we traveled to the West Coast, Guam, the Philippines, and Hong Kong. After all, we did need to keep an eye on the Russians. And they felt likewise about us.

The submarine I served on, the USS Tautog, *sailing off the coast of Oahu, Hawaii, with Diamond Head crater in the background*

After six years as a sailor, I decided to muster out and get a college education. Arizona State University was my choice for two reasons. First, the state of Arizona is covered in telescopes. It is dry and clear, so the stars are beautiful and there is a lot to see. Second, two of my shipmates, P. J. Boyle and Ray Frazier, were going to attend that same university and we could share expenses. Oh yes, and we could also party together. One of those was more important than the other, but I don't remember the order right now.

I started out at ASU to be a professional astronomer, but it did not work out as planned. I quickly found that many astronomers were mathematicians who wanted to measure the universe, not look at it. Twice I traveled to Kitt Peak National Observatory, near Tucson, to help one of the professors. It was made clear to me that there was no place to look through those instruments; they simply gathered data for later analysis. But I did not want to take measurements; I wanted to look for myself.

The most fun I had with astronomy at ASU was as a teaching aide in the astronomy lab. We set up telescopes and showed folks the sky from the top of the physics building. It certainly was not dark, but we could view the Moon and planets. It helped to introduce other students to what they were learning about in the beginning astronomy courses.

But I was frustrated, so I changed my major course of study to communications. This included courses in journalism, radio, and television. It all turned out for the best. Learning to write clearly and concisely is a skill that proved worthwhile almost right away.

Answering an advertisement in the Sunday paper, I wound up with a job at the DeVry Institute of Technology in Phoenix. As a professor there for twenty-six years, I trained many technicians. These students graduated from DeVry and had their opportunity to travel around the world, raise a family, and enjoy life. I am proud of that. Many of the astronomical adventures in this book were undertaken while I was a professor at DeVry. The money I made and the time off I enjoyed made it all possible.

My first telescope was an eight-inch Newtonian, a simple scope that is easy to care for and I found fun to use. It uses a carefully polished mirror at the bottom of a tube that reflects the light to another mirror that bounces the light out to the observer's eye. This mirror configuration was invented by Isaac Newton over three hundred years ago, but a good design is still a good design.

The eight-inch Newtonian with me trying to figure what I am going to observe that night

The other thing that got me on the track toward really enjoying my time out under dark skies was joining an astronomy club. The Saguaro Astronomy Club (SAC) in Phoenix is filled with people who just love to get out under dark skies and view the universe. It was great to have a chance to discuss telescopes, eyepieces, objects to view, and places to travel with my fellow club members. Many of them became lifelong friends and observing buddies.

SAC members at the VLA radio telescope in New Mexico

Writing some observing articles for the Saguaro Astronomy Club newsletter started me down a path that led to this book. I called the articles in the SAC newsletter "What's Up." The name was both a pointer to the sky above and a tribute to Bugs Bunny.

David Eicher was a teenager in the Midwest, and his enthusiasm for observing led him to start *Deep Sky Magazine*. I was fortunate enough to write and publish many articles for *Deep Sky*. Also, Bob Kepple and Glen Sanner started a set of magazines that covered one constellation per issue, exactly the way I generally keep my observations and logs. Years later they published the *Night Sky Observing Guide,* a set of three large-volume books that cover most of the objects an observer would see with a modest telescope. I am very proud to be the largest contributor to that project.

Tom and Jeannie Clark started *Amateur Astronomy Magazine* to provide information about what was not being covered in the major magazines. I revived the name "What's Up" to use in this magazine, and the articles were well received for over five years.

Springer Publishing contacted me during this time, and we discussed my writing a book. After a year of putting some observations, tips, and techniques together, my first book was published. It is called *Deep Sky Observing*, and it hit the market in the year 2000.

At about this same time, I completed my largest observing list. When *Burnham's Celestial Handbook* became available in the 1980s I bought my first set of these books at the Riverside Telescope Makers conference. I immediately saw what an excellent job the late Robert Burnham had done by compiling a list of great objects to view and plenty of data about them. I started using *Burnham's* as my observing list. After fourteen years of dedicated effort I was able to say that I have viewed all the deep-sky objects in those books.

Springer Publishing contacted me about doing a second book, this one in their Advanced Amateur Series. That book took more time than the first, as I had to figure out how much scientific information to include and how much would be purely my observations. After nearly two years, *Nebulae and How to Observe Them* hit the market in 2006.

Most recently, I have been writing yet another set of "What's Up" articles. They are available on the Internet on the website www. cloudynights.com—just look under the menu "articles" and then "monthly." I have made my way around the sky once, so there are over sixty articles. They cover many of my favorite deep-sky objects, and I am starting to go around again and write about things I missed or did not have room for the first time.

Many would say that writing two books and over 150 articles should be enough for one lifetime. I would agree if I were not obsessed, and I am willing to admit that I am obsessed.

Okay, I am bragging ... enough is enough.

Each chapter within this book contains observations made on a particular night. First I will discuss what led up to that night and what I saw and learned as I made progress toward being a better observer of the sky. I hope that my story will show you some tricks you might not understand right now and will still be entertaining. We do live in a world that must be entertained.

The first night I will discuss is November 10, 1979, very early along my pathway to the stars. I was using the eight-inch Newtonian at Four Peaks Road, about fifty miles from central Phoenix, near Saguaro Lake. It was not dark, but conditions were good enough to see some Milky Way.

Bill Anderson was along for the evening and was taking some photos while I did some visual observing. First up was the Double Cluster in Perseus. This famous grouping of two bright clusters was perfect for using my new eyepiece, a 40mm with a wide field of view for that time.

The designations for the two clusters are NGC 884 and NGC 869. On this night they were easily seen with the naked eye and elongated east-west. Using the 10X50 binoculars I could see six stars resolved in the two clusters. The wide view of the binoculars showed a curved chain of stars that trailed off from the north side. Moving to the eight-inch scope with the wide-field 40mm eyepiece showed twenty-eight stars counted in NGC 869. It was very bright, very large, and pretty compressed. An easily seen dark lane ran through the cluster and cut it into one-third, two-third parts. The other cluster, NGC 884, showed twenty-seven stars counted and was bright, very large, rich in stars, and compressed and displayed several orange stars involved.

The Double Cluster, shot with a 200mm lens

During this time, I was just starting to find my way around the Messier list. Charles Messier was an eighteenth-century French comet hunter. He began a list of objects in the sky that looked enough like comets in his simple telescope to be confused with a new comet. Because his scopes were pretty modest instruments, all he could see were the brightest objects in the sky. So an "M" object is always going to be bright compared to other clusters, galaxies, or nebulae.

Messier 52 is a star cluster in the constellation of Cassiopeia. With the eight-inch and a 20mm eyepiece it is bright, large, rich, and not compressed. I saw it as well detached from the Milky Way background. At higher magnification with a 12mm eyepiece I counted forty-five stars in the cluster; the brightest star on the west side was light orange in color. This cluster included a ring of pretty bright stars that made this cluster interesting.

A drawing of M 52 with the eight-inch and a 12mm eyepiece

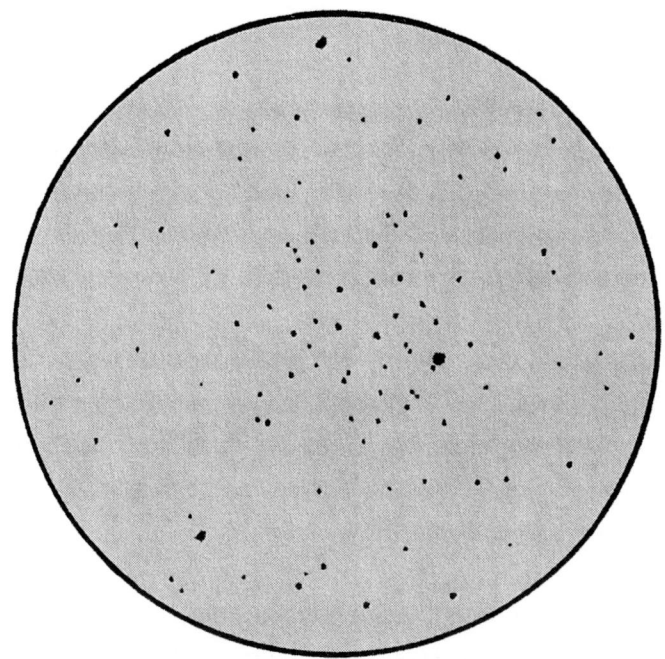

I was getting interested in double stars, an interest that would grow quite a lot over the years. This night I was searching for Eta Cassiopeiae. I spent some time with the star map so I could find its location within the stars of Cassiopeia. Once it was in the field of view of the telescope, I raised the power to 135X to split the pair of stars. This higher power let me see that this was indeed a double star. After observing for a few moments I saw that the colors of the two stars were yellow and light orange. This pair had good color contrast, and I found those colors very interesting.

The colors of stars indicate differences in the temperature of the star. In the same way that a piece of metal changes color as you heat it—red, yellow, and then blue-white as the temperature goes up—the color of a star is determined by the temperature. Red and orange stars are cool, blue stars are hot, and yellow (like our Sun) falls in the middle.

This is just the first of the evenings (and one day) that we will explore in this book. At this point in my time as an observer of the universe, I was just learning the skills needed to find my way among the stars. Many of the names were still difficult, and determining where even bright clusters and galaxies were located could take some time.

In the face of all that, when I did find a new object to view it was thrilling. I wondered if double stars contained other observers looking back at me. How would the sky look from inside one of those clusters of stars? If you could stand the cold, how huge would Jupiter be from one of its satellites?

Between the human imagination and the facts about the universe, there was much to see and learn. I was anxious to get on with it.

Chapter 2: September 26, 1981

ᝣᶬᕼ

Twin Arrows, Arizona

The eight-inch (200mm) Newtonian was an enjoyable scope, and I saw a lot with it over the three years I owned it. Then I caught a disease called "aperture fever." This is the incessant need for a larger telescope. One of the symptoms of this fever is the illusion of a little voice in your head that says, "If you had a bigger scope, you would see so much more." Okay, I listened to the voice. I sold the eight-inch and shopped for a way to build a larger scope.

I had a chance to visit the Coulter Optical workshop and see rows of automated grinding machines making mirrors by the dozens. In my opinion, it is a noisy and difficult task that I have never taken on. I am more than willing to work for the money so that someone much more qualified than me can grind and polish the mirror in my telescope.

With that in mind I ordered a 17.5-inch (450mm) mirror from Coulter Optical. During the wait for the mirror to be available I started planning how to put that big mirror into a workable telescope. I settled on a simple mount that is similar to a navy gun mount. It moves up and down or left and right. Many people apply John Dobson's name to this design and call it a Dobsonian. The good news is that they are easy to build and maintain.

I bought a large piece of tubular cardboard used in construction as a concrete form to make pillars. One brand name is Sonotube. This large tube would be contained within a plywood box that held the scope together with the mirror resting on a trap door at the rear end. First I needed to get the tubing within the box. This proved more difficult than I first thought.

*A friend on the roof of my house using a hammer to
encourage the box to slide down the Sonotube*

Once the hammer proved to have little effect, he started using his foot to pound the tube into place. I never did convince him to stand on top and jump up and down. Eventually the tube was in place within the plywood box. I have no doubts that my neighbors were ready to call an ambulance.

My friend using his foot as a hammer

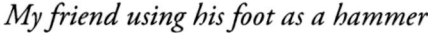

The trap door feature at the back end of the telescope

At one point I opened the trap door at the exact angle to hit myself in the face with a hot beam of Arizona sunlight from that very shiny mirror. It took at least an hour for my face to cool off. I cannot recommend it as a quick tanning device.

The complete telescope before painting

Notice the elongated hole that the focuser sits into. We made a poor measurement of some kind and had to widen the opening to get the focuser in the correct location. I later added a black piece of cardboard to cover the embarrassing hole in the tube. Other than that, the scope turned out just like I hoped it would.

The good thing about owning a large telescope is that it will show you lots of detail within deep-sky objects that are difficult or impossible with a smaller scope. The obvious disadvantage is that it is a larger device and that makes it tougher to move around and set up for the night's viewing session. The other problem is light pollution.

Light pollution is the glow of light that all cities create. Porch lights, athletic fields, advertising, and street lights create a dome of light that can be seen for many miles in all directions. The only way to see clear, dark sky is to drive far from the lights of the city.

Paul Maxson was a SAC member for many years and today takes excellent images of the Sun and planets from his backyard in the little city of Surprise, Arizona. In 1981 his parents owned a parcel of land about thirty-five miles from Flagstaff at an area called Twin Arrows. There was nothing around in any direction that would shine direct lighting onto our observing site—just what you want. It would be my first trip to truly dark sky.

The weather for September 26, 1981, was perfect. There were no clouds, and the sky was clear and dark. The phase of the Moon was new, and New Moon means no Moon, just what is needed to see lots of stars far from the city lights. Paul and I dropped off sleeping bags and other necessities at his parents' cabin nearby and started setting up the telescope in a field that would give us a clear view of the night sky in all directions.

Paul (left) and me with the 17.5-inch telescope, ready for a great night

We got all the equipment ready and sat down to eat a sandwich just as the Sun was setting. Once we finished the sandwiches the sky started getting dark and stars were filling the sky from horizon to horizon. The bright swath of the Milky Way was more and more obvious as the twilight gave way to dark sky. The Milky Way is an edge-on view of the galaxy we live in. Lots of stars, star clusters, and nebulae are visible within our beautiful galaxy.

One of my favorite star clusters was available right away–Messier 11. M 11 was easy to view, bright, and obvious. This cluster of stars was also very compressed. This means that the stars were all very close together. At 135X in the new 17.5-inch telescope this cluster was very rich in stars and there was a "V" shape seen easily. Many years ago Admiral Smyth spoke of this feature as looking like a flight of wild ducks. This cluster appeared sliced to pieces by dark lanes that wound among all these stars. It is a unique cluster and has always been a favorite of mine.

An image of M 11 by Chris Schur

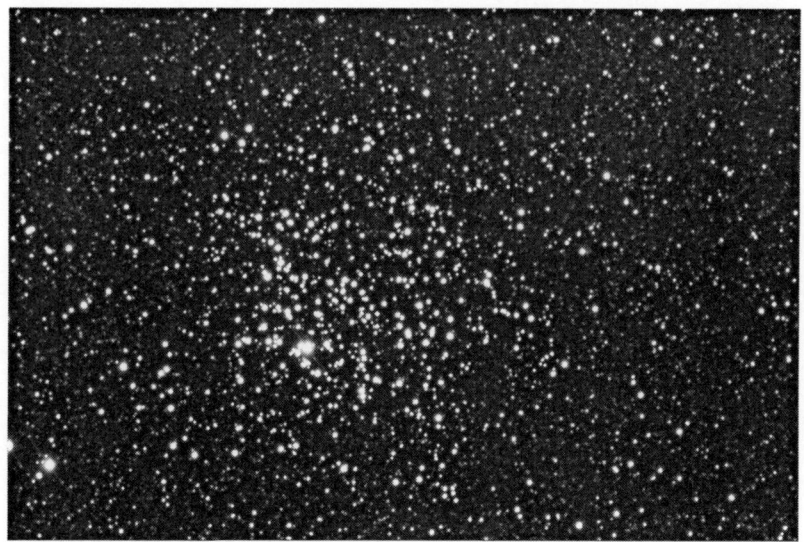

M 17 is a nebula. The Latin plural is nebulae. These are huge clouds of dust and gas that are lit up by the stars embedded within them. Just like a neon lamp glows from the electric current passing through it, a nebula will glow from the ultraviolet radiation emitted from the energetic stars within the gas cloud. These bright nebulae are the places where stars are born. The gas and dust is compressed within the nebulous cloud, and eventually a nuclear fusion reaction starts within the core and the star begins to shine.

Using the big reflector at 100X, M 17 was very bright and large and showed an irregular shape. This nebula has received a variety of names over the years. The Swan section is the brightest and most obvious section on the south side. I have also heard this called the Checkmark. This bright area of the nebula displayed several dark lanes that pass in front of the bright glow and cut it into pieces. Using a telescope this large, 100X is fairly low power, so the nebula was afloat in a rich Milky Way field of stars. There were eighteen stars seen as embedded within the nebulous glow.

M 17

NGC 6543 is a planetary nebula in the constellation of Draco. A planetary nebula is a gas cloud emitted by a star at the end of its life. Stars the size of our Sun do not explode after they have lived for billions of years; they puff off the outer layers of the star and form this type of nebula. Often the core of the star is seen at the center of the disk of dust and gas.

The NGC designation stands for New General Catalog. A gentleman named J.L.E. Dreyer was putting together the largest observing list ever made for the largest telescope ever made, a seventy-two-inch huge telescope built in Ireland in the middle of the nineteenth century. It was called the Leviathan of Parsonstown. He published the NGC in 1888, and it became the most complete list of deep-sky objects in its time. The NGC is still very useful today, and many of the objects I will discuss in this book are from the NGC.

Using the 17.5-inch scope at 320X, NGC 6543 showed a bright disk that I saw as elongated in a ratio of 1.8X1. The central star could be seen at all magnifications. There was much detail within the disk. Two brighter curved areas gave the impression of spiral structure.

The very center of the nebulosity included the central star, and a donut-shaped area around that was darker than the disk. This gave the impression that the star was within a cavity in the disk.

NGC-6543

Messier 2 is a globular cluster. When we looked at M 11 earlier, it was an open cluster. The difference in these two types of clusters is pretty easy to spot in the telescope. Open clusters contain from a dozen to several hundred stars and are always found along the path of the Milky Way. Globular clusters contain over a thousand to possibly a million stars and form their characteristic globe shape.

M 2 is the showpiece of the constellation Aquarius. This globular was easy to spot in the little 10X50 finder scope. All large telescopes need some type of finder scope that shows a wide field of view and has crosshairs within to show where the main scope is pointing. If an object can be seen in the finder scope, then it is bright.

M 2 showed bright, very large, round, and very bright in the middle at 100X in the 17.5-inch telescope. At 250X there were twelve stars resolved in the compact central core region and a profusion of hundreds of stars in the outer corona. All these stars were superimposed on an unresolved background haze of stars. Lovely chains of stars meandered outward from the bright core, and several dark lanes were visible within the cluster.

M 2

M 74 rose above the eastern horizon as the night progressed, and I was impressed with how much I could see of it in the new telescope. With the power at 220X there was a wealth of detail to be seen in this distant galaxy. I was able to see a stellar core and spiral structure with two arms winding out from the central hub. These curved arms, filled with stars and nebulae, were immediately evident. The arms were very mottled, a condition that makes bright objects show a texture. I saw it as elongated bright and dark regions within the galaxy.

M 74

After observing for several hours, we sat down for a rest and just stared at the beauty of the night sky; the path of the Milky Way from Sagittarius to Cassiopeia; the brilliance of the stars; and that feeling of peace that getting in touch with nature will bring.

Twin Arrows

I love the universe; I think it loves me back.

Chapter 3: May 26, 1984

Riverside Telescope Makers Conference

I will admit right up front that I am a social person; I really enjoy getting together with a group of astronomers and chatting about viewing the sky. If we are talking about objects we have seen, the latest eyepieces, or a new scope that someone has purchased, it is all good.

One of the most fun places to do this is the Riverside Telescope Makers Conference (RTMC). It has been held for decades at the Big Bear Lake scout camp in California. There is plenty of room for lots of astronomers to gather. This location is about an eight-hour drive from Phoenix, and we often go in a caravan and chat on the CB radio to keep us all awake.

Because it is always on the Memorial Day weekend, we are driving the opposite of the traffic on the I-10 freeway. As Los Angeles is emptying out we are driving toward the city. Once the conference is over and people are coming back toward LA, we are driving east. It is fun to watch the huge traffic jam when it is going the other way.

Just as I did for the rest of the book, I will concentrate on one day and night, but there have been lots of great times at RTMC over the years. This particular day, I was one of the speakers at RTMC; my topic was a tracking mount we built as a Saguaro Astronomy

Club project. It is a pretty simple device that will allow you to take wide-angle astrophotos.

The talk was quite successful, and there were lots of questions when I finished. Cliff Holmes asked me to make room for the next speaker by taking the device and the rest of the questions outside. At least a dozen interested folks follow me out to have a good look at the tracker and ask some more questions. Cliff later told me that he had rarely seen so much interest in such a device. I was happy to hear that we might have sparked lots of other folks to build a tracker. It is essentially two wooden boards with a carefully placed hinge and a threaded rod that moves the upper board and camera at the rate the stars move overhead. I bought the tripod from Celestron at RTMC. There are plans for an updated version of the tracker on the club website: www.saguaroastro.org.

The tracker in the updated form

The type of image that is pretty easy to shoot with the tracker. It is a four-minute exposure with a 35mm lens of the area near the center of the Milky Way galaxy. The bright star on the right side is Antares. In the center is the dark nebula called the Pipe. There is a small meteor just to the left of the Pipe nebula, and the Lagoon nebula is to the left of the meteor.

There are several really good things to be said about going to an astronomy conference. One of them is a chance to look at, and look through, some excellent telescopes. It is always encouraging to see what others have done. This particular occasion there was a beautiful eighteen-inch scope made by Kevin Medlock. This telescope got me to thinking about using a "truss tube." This means that the tube is not a solid piece but can be taken apart and stored or transported more easily. More on this later.

Kevin Medlock's eighteen-inch scope

It not only looked good, but the views in it were excellent. Kevin was kind enough to be taking requests, and we pointed the scope at the edge-on galaxy, NGC 4565 in Coma Berenices. At 135X it was very bright, very large, and extremely elongated (10X1) and had a very bright middle. The dark lane was easy to see. Raising the power to 200X showed some fine detail within the dark lane in moments of good seeing, and there were tiny light and dark areas within the central lane. A stellar nucleus was just below the dark lane.

Remember that the close-up shots in this book are from Chris Schur. This one was taken with his twelve-inch Newtonian. The original photo was on film and then later scanned into his computer.

There is one thing that will become obvious if you spend some time at RTMC. I am speaking of the difference between observers and telescopes makers. It is rare for one person to demonstrate both types of personalities. The names say it all: "observers" want to look at the sky in all its glory. If they build a telescope, it will be used for many years. There may be a few accessories added, as we are all looking for something nifty to help us enjoy observing more. "Telescope makers" are just that. They want to build telescopes. Once the finishing touches have been put on that scope, they are ready to start the next telescope so they can apply what they learned while constructing this one. Telescope makers know enough of the sky to be able to test that newly completed scope. Rarely do they wish to spend lots of hours at the eyepiece; telescope makers would rather be in the machine shop fabricating nifty parts.

With all that in mind, when the telescope makers show up at Riverside they want to point the scope at something that is easily found in the sky. Two objects come to mind immediately—the Ring Nebula and M 13, the Hercules Cluster. The Ring Nebula is a planetary nebula in the constellation of Lyra, the lyre. Messier 13 is a big globular cluster in the constellation of Hercules, the Hero. Remember that these clusters contain many hundreds of thousands of stars and form a globe shape. My friends and I have spent many hours walking around the telescope field and seen these two objects in many telescopes. We will return to the Ring Nebula later; right now let's look at M 13.

At 100X in the 17.5-inch telescope M 13 was very bright, very large, well resolved, much brighter in the middle, and little elongated 1.2X1 in an east-west direction. The most prominent chains were off the north and south sides, with many silvery stars in front of a sparkling globe in the background. Moving to 250X showed the best view. I counted forty-six stars in the northwest quadrant; most were silver, and a few were yellow or light orange. There was a chain of nine stars running across the core from east to west.

There is a famous dark feature within M 13. It is three lanes that form a propeller, or "Y" shape. The dark "propeller" feature is held with direct vision as small, thin dark lines near the core. I can only see the propeller on the best nights.

A shot from Chris Schur just showing a hint of
the Propeller near the core at the top

Besides a chance to hear people talk about telescopes and observing, RTMC offers a big swap meet. There is often plenty of great stuff for sale. I came this year with several things on my shopping list. First was a nebular filter. This is a filter that will allow the passage of light that is given off by nebulae. It filters out the light from streetlights and allows through the light from glowing clouds in space. In 1984 they were pretty rare, and I had managed only one view through one of these filters—but I was hooked. When I purchased mine, I was told that one of the objects it would work best on was the Veil Nebula in Cygnus. What a great tip!

The Veil Nebula is a supernova remnant. This is the gas that was blown into space by a gigantic stellar explosion. It turns out the really big stars, dozens of times larger than the Sun, blow up at the end of their life.

NGC 6992 is the brightest portion of the Veil Nebula. This was created by a supernova about thirty thousand years ago, and we just happen to be lucky enough to live while it is visible. This very elongated glow is amazing in the 17.5-inch with a 20mm Erfle eyepiece and a nebula filter. Only about one-quarter of this glowing strand of nebulosity can fit into the field of view, and the scope must be scanned to see all that is available. NGC 6992 has loops and swirls of nebulosity that give a three-dimensional effect. It looks like a strand of taffy with stars embedded in it. The nebula makes such a difference that we called the device the "Veil Nebula Filter" for some time after first acquiring one. They work on lots of other nebulae around the sky, but the Veil still provides the best detail with the filter in place.

Veil Nebula

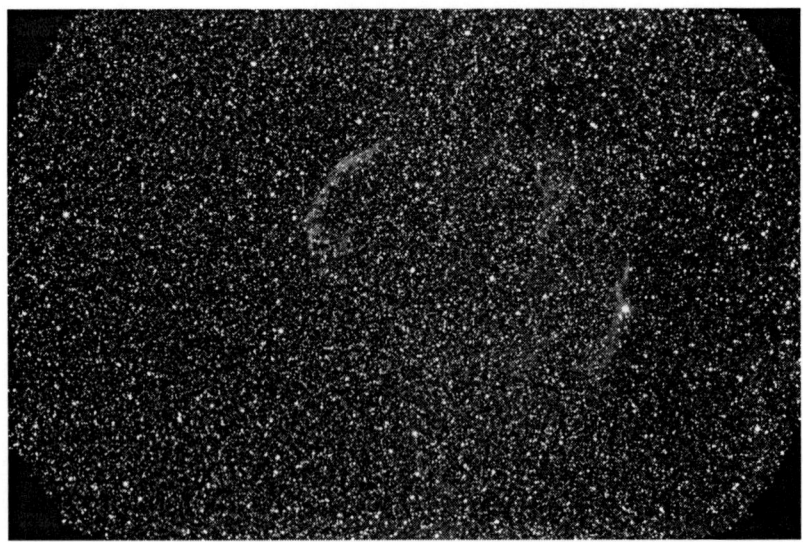

There are two other things I acquired while at RTMC this time; both are military hardware. The first was an old finder, called the M-17. It had a 50mm (two-inch) aperture and showed just over five degrees of sky. It was perfect for a finder scope. The other was a huge, wide-field eyepiece. It was a 38mm focal length eyepiece that used to go on the periscope of a Sherman tank, so we called it "the tank eyepiece." It was big enough to deserve that name. Bill Anderson was nice enough to machine me a fitting so it would slide into a two-inch focuser. I used both items for many years.

I am fortunate enough to have as one of my astronomical buddies David Fredericksen. He makes his way to Riverside virtually every year. Early on we drove over in two vehicles so that I had room for a telescope. To keep awake and alert we would chat on the CB radio as we drove through the night. More recently we have not been doing as much telescope building, and so Dave is nice enough to drive and we chip in for gas. It makes the trip go more quickly to chat about observing times in the past and what we are hoping to buy at the swap meet.

One other thing that going to a conference will provide you is a chance to use a type of telescope you have never used before. There were two gentlemen who set up solar telescopes and allowed people to observe detail on our star. There are features on the Sun called prominences; they are huge streamers of gas that the Sun is ejecting. They change their shape within ten or fifteen minutes and are fascinating to watch. The bad news is that you must have a very specialized telescope and/or filter to view these prominences. I have never had the money and inclination to purchase a solar scope, but maybe one of these days I will. It was lots of fun to look through one provided by a generous astronomer at RTMC.

Often many of the SAC members would drive over to see what was going on at Riverside. Here is a photo from 1981 of the club members in front of my scope. I am the guy with the big hair and mustache in the middle. It was always nice to see a friendly face at the conference, and you could show off what you just found at a terrific price during the swap meet.

The RTMC solar scope

As I said when discussing Kevin Medlock's eighteen-inch telescope, I was intrigued by the idea of a truss tube. As we discussed it among ourselves I really wanted to give one a try. My first attempt was rather poor; I had made the aluminum struts too long and too flimsy. The second time I decided to create three boxes connected by struts. This is the form in which I used the scope for about two years.

My appearance on the cover of Telescope Making *magazine #26 with the 17.5-inch in its "three box" configuration. Sharp-eyed viewers will notice the old M-17 finder scope near the eyepiece.*

TELESCOPE**26**

MAKING

ISSN 0190-5570

The magazine *for, by,* and *about* telescope makers!   Summer 1985

I had always found the 17.5-inch f/4.5 telescope to have mediocre optics, and I wanted a sharper image with a large telescope. Well, the universe supplied me with John Hall. He had always been grinding telescopes and had a variety of mirrors in telescopes all around Arizona. He offered me an eighteen-inch f/6 mirror at a reasonable price, and I jumped at it. The 17.5-inch was sold within a week. By the way, John later moved to Texas and he and his son created Pegasus Optics.

I knew that any solid tube eighteen-inch telescope would be huge, and I thought I could build a truss tube scope that would be easier to handle. Well, maybe "easier to handle," but not easy to handle. Any method you use to construct a telescope with a fifty-two-pound mirror that is nine feet (three meters) tall, you are going to have a big scope. And it was.

But the views in it were excellent. Visually, it is still the best telescope I have ever owned. However, it was also difficult to take out and get set up. Often David Fredericksen was nice enough to help, and it still took forty-five minutes of hot, sweaty work to get it all bolted together. Once it was together and collimated (the mirrors aligned to give the best images), this scope was a beauty.

My eighteen-inch telescope

I am going to leave you in suspense about what I did to replace this scope. Next we are off to Australia.

CHAPTER 4: APRIL 11, 1986

ᴄᴍ

FIRST AUSTRALIA TRIP

It all started with an advertisement in *Sky and Telescope* magazine. An Australian gentleman wanted to correspond with others interested in viewing and photographing the night sky. This is my kind of guy. I know, in the world of instant e-mail and Facebook communication, that this next line will be a shock: I took out a piece of paper and wrote complete sentences on it. Then I put it in an envelope (with some extra postage) and mailed it to Australia. Within a week it was there.

That is how I first got in touch with Jim Barclay. We wrote back and forth several times, and then I decided to phone him. I calculated that midnight in Arizona is about five o'clock in the afternoon in Brisbane, Queensland, Australia. I also got clear that the call would be about one dollar per minute. So I made a list of what to chat about and tried to stick to the list. It was lots of fun to write to and chat with Jim, and we formed a friendship from a very long distance.

At about this time the magazine *Deep Sky Observing Guide* was getting started. We decided to combine our northern and southern observations in some constellations that are available to both our observing sites. We viewed Hydra, Centaurus, and Orion. Then we put together our observations and got them published in the magazine. It was fun, and this collaboration strengthened our overseas bond.

Over the years I have become convinced of the fact that the universe has a rather bizarre sense of humor. With that in mind, I was still somewhat shocked to find out that my observing buddy, AJ Crayon, had also been writing with Jim Barclay. Unbeknownst to each other we had both become "pen pals" with this Australian astronomer. Weird, man, weird.

By now the 1986 passage of Halley's Comet was growing closer and we realized that this famous object would be at its best from south of the equator. Jim and his wife, Lynn, were kind enough to offer us a chance to stay at their house and observe the big event.

The airline tickets were not cheap, but this was a once-in-a-lifetime event. David Fredericksen, Chris Schur, and I got our tickets and started planning what to take along. Chris built a small mount that we could fit in our luggage. He carried some of it and I took the motor and a few tools in my bag. Obviously the camera was carry-on luggage.

I also carried on board my 10X50 binoculars. Allow me to digress for a moment and talk about binoculars. A good pair of binoculars is the easiest to use and simplest to carry piece of astronomical viewing equipment. The beautiful wide field of view that binoculars can provide will captivate you.

The "10X50" given above means that these binoculars have 50mm (two-inch) objectives; that is the size of the glass lenses in the front of the binoculars. The "10X" designation means just what it looks like—these binoculars provide ten times magnification. That means the view will appear as if you walked ten times closer to the target and viewed it from there. I find that a pair of binoculars of this size and magnification is the largest I can hand hold and see a steady view of the sky.

So either buy a good pair of binoculars or break out those that have been just sitting in the closet for years, clean them off and start viewing the sky. It is a great way to start your observing. I also take mine out every time and I have been viewing the sky for thirty-three years. After all this time I still dearly love to lean back in a comfy chair and scan along the Milky Way with a good pair of binoculars. There is no other view like it.

Okay, back to the Australian trip. The flight was fourteen hours long but was worth it. We sat together and planned what to view and photograph. Then we took a nap and then we ate. And ... we were halfway there. We landed in Sydney, sat around in the airport, and then had another two-hour plane flight to Brisbane, where Jim and Lynn resided. They were actually in a small beach community called Caloundra. It was far enough away from the big city of Brisbane to have quite dark skies in their backyard.

Once we were finished mugging for the camera, we waited for it to get dark. Oh, those southern skies. Seeing them for the first time was amazing, and a little disorienting. We saw proof right away that we were not in Arizona any more. From Arizona, the brightest star, Sirius, never gets more than forty degrees above the southern horizon. Once it got dark enough to start recognizing a few of the brightest objects, we saw Sirius straight overhead. Wow!

I picked up the binoculars, had a seat in a folding chair, and started scanning this new sky. Having the constellations of Canis Major and Puppis straight up was one thing, but now Centaurus, Vela, and Crux were following it across the sky. The Milky Way was stunning; it showed huge bright areas divided up by obvious dark lanes. Viewing through the binoculars showed a wide variety of star clusters involved with bright and dark nebulae.

The group in Australia. In order from right to left are Chris Schur, David Fredericksen, Jim Barclay, and me. Obviously David and I decided to buy "slatch hats." Chris brought the cowboy hat for Jim. It all seemed a good idea at the time. Behind us is Jim's observatory with the 12.5-inch f/6 Newtonian. The Australian flag has a representation of the Southern Cross and Alpha Centauri.

A sixteenth-century mapmaker named Johannes Bayer started the convention of using Greek letters as designations for the brightest stars. So "Alpha Centauri" is the brightest star in Centaurus, "Beta Centauri" is the second, and so on. His method is so ingrained it is still in use today.

Using this method, Omega Centauri is the twenty-fourth brightest star in the constellation of the Centaur. But this is not a star. It is the brightest globular cluster in the sky, one of the few deep-sky objects that can be seen with the naked eye. It is bright in the binoculars and shows immediately that it is not a star because it appears as a fuzzy ball of light.

Moving up to the 12.5-inch telescope provided an amazing view. It was very bright, extremely large, extremely rich in stars, and very compressed. What can be said about the king of the globular clusters? This fantastic object is overwhelming from southern latitudes. The globular filled the field at 140X; there were chains of stars that meandered outward in all directions from a blazing core.

A photo taken by Jim Barclay of Omega Centauri. It was taken with the 12.5-inch Newtonian and is a forty-minute exposure on Ilford film.

Modern studies have found that this huge ball of stars is not a globular cluster at all. Omega Centauri is the core of what used to be a galaxy separate from the Milky Way. Many hundreds of millions of years ago this galaxy passed close enough to the Milky Way to go into orbit around our galaxy. As the millennia progressed, this small galaxy had its arms pulled away by the gravitation force of the Milky Way, and all that is left is the core we see today.

NGC 4755 is an open cluster of stars in Crux, the Southern Cross. It is more commonly called "the Jewel Box" because it contains several stars with obvious color. This cluster can be seen with the naked eye as a bright spot in the Milky Way, located to the left of the Southern Cross. In the 12.5-inch Newtonian scope it was a "wow" object if there ever was one. It was pretty large, compressed, and rich in stars. I counted eighty-one stars involved using a 40mm wide-angle eyepiece. The most obvious feature was three stars in a straight line that were almost in the center of the cluster. I saw these three stars as yellow and blue and then dark orange with lots of brilliant color. The cluster also contained another five stars, which I saw as yellow and light orange in color—a truly unique object.

A photo of the Jewel Box cluster from Jim Barclay. It is a twenty-five-minute exposure with the 12.5-inch scope.

We were happily surprised at the fact that so many people were interested in what we were doing and wanted to know more about our trip "Down Under." Jan Sprogis and Martin Spencer are the only two names I remember, but we had several backyard barbeque parties so Jim could show off his American visitors.

Our appearance on the cover of the local newspaper, showing the mount that Chris brought along to take photos. David (right) and I are looking up, I guess trying to find Comet Halley while Chris is adjusting the mount.

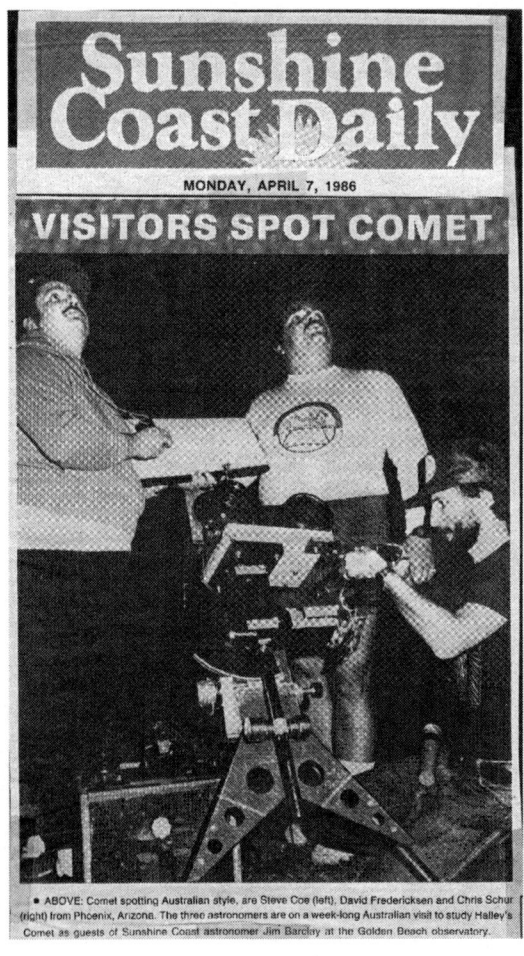

Sunshine Coast Daily

MONDAY, APRIL 7, 1986

VISITORS SPOT COMET

● ABOVE: Comet spotting Australian style, are Steve Coe (left), David Fredericksen and Chris Schur (right) from Phoenix, Arizona. The three astronomers are on a week-long Australian visit to study Halley's Comet as guests of Sunshine Coast astronomer Jim Barclay at the Golden Beach observatory.

Let's discuss comets in general before we get to the specifics of Halley's Comet. When the solar system was forming, about 4.5 billion years ago, it was spinning on its axis. As it did that it formed a shape much like a pancake with a bulge in the middle. The central bulge became the Sun, and most of the dust and gas left over got pulled in by gravity to form the planets and major satellites within the solar system.

But all the material did not get used up. Some of the leftover dust and gas formed comets. Comets move around the Sun in elongated orbits, which means that they only pass within view of people on Earth at rare intervals. As their orbits take them near to the Sun, the comet forms a tail from the material that boils off the comet because of the heat of the Sun. Most of the time they are far from the Sun and Earth; at these far-flung locations the temperatures are hundreds of degrees below zero and all the material of the comet is frozen solid.

Specifically, Comet Halley has an orbit that takes about seventy-six years to complete one ellipse around the Sun. I have to say "about" because the planets can pull on the core of the comet and move it around. This gravity effect changes the exact time it takes to complete one orbit.

For seventy-five years of its orbital loop, the comet's nucleus is a frozen ball of ice and dust. Some of it is water ice; some is carbon dioxide. There are also some other minerals and gases within the comet nucleus. As it comes inside the orbit of Mars, on its way toward the Sun, the heat will boil away the gas and dust. This forms the "coma," a sphere of gas and dust around the central nucleus. This coma is much larger than the nucleus and reflects lots of light. Therefore it becomes much easier to see the comet in a telescope.

When enough of this coma is created it starts to trail some of it behind the comet, and this forms the tail. Tails are the most prominent feature of comets, and anyone who knows anything about comets knows that they form tails. There are two types of tail: dust and ion. Dust tails are just what you would think; they have a consistency somewhat like cigarette smoke, formed by the dust from the nucleus. The ion tail is formed by the chemical molecules in the gas. As the powerful ultraviolet light of the Sun strikes these molecules ions are created. An ion is a charged particle. Because the tails are such light materials the solar wind pushes the tail in a direction away from the Sun.

We had seen Comet Halley from Arizona before we left. It was just seen by the naked eye, and we saw that it had formed a modest tail. The main reason for this is that it is "underneath" Scorpius from our position, so it will never rise above the horizon by more than about ten degrees.

To be perfectly honest, I used Comet Halley as an excuse to get off work for a week and travel to Australia. I had the time off saved up, but I do thank Bill Sears, my dean at DeVry Institute, for giving in to my astronomical dreams.

Jim Barclay has a big pair of binoculars, 15X80 in size. We leaned them against the edge of the dome to get them stable. Once you had these heavy binoculars in a place where they were steady, the view of the comet was excellent, easily the best view of a comet I had had up to this point in my observing career. It was bright and much larger than the 3.5 degree field of the big binoculars. The core was very bright, and the coma was about one degree in size with a bright tail to the west. There were four (!) levels of condensation to the head of the comet and an obvious bright jet of material (the ion tail) that passed down the center of the wider dust tail—a terrific view.

Moving up to the 12.5-inch f/6 Newtonian at 300X there were two very bright jets of material boiling off the nucleus to either side (northwest–southeast) and curving back along the path of the tail. These fountains were easily seen at this high power in the big scope.

It turned out that the photographic mount that Chris Schur traveled with did a fine job. We shot many photos of Comet Halley.

A set of drawings I made. The top one was made with the binoculars and the bottom drawing was made at the 12.5-inch scope.

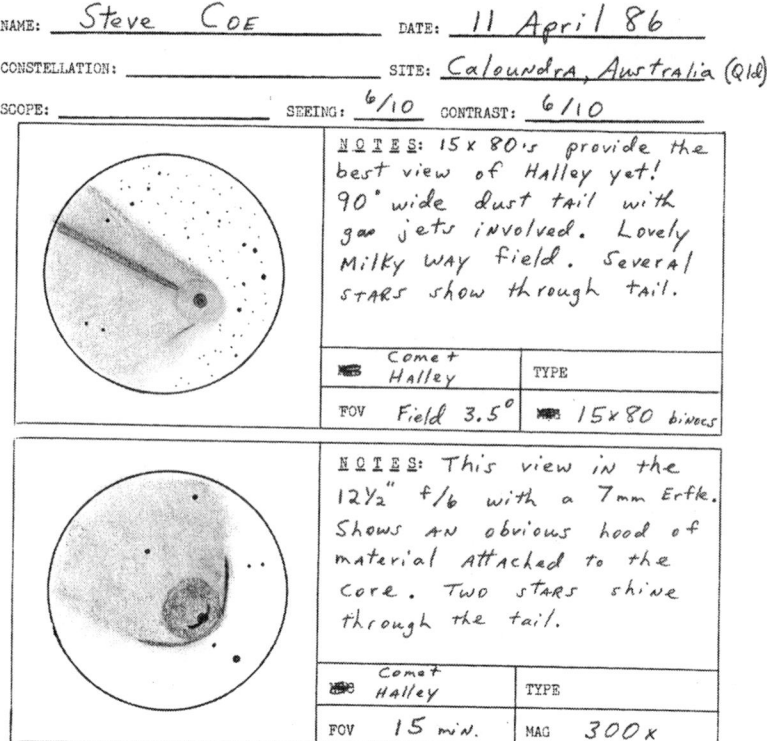

NAME: _Steve Coe_   DATE: _11 April 86_

CONSTELLATION: _____   SITE: _Caloundra, Australia (Qld)_

SCOPE: _____   SEEING: _6/10_   CONTRAST: _6/10_

NOTES: 15 x 80's provide the best view of Halley yet! 90° wide dust tail with gas jets involved. Lovely Milky Way field. Several stars show through tail.

Comet Halley	TYPE
FOV Field 3.5°	15 x 80 binocs

NOTES: This view in the 12½" f/6 with a 7mm Erfle. Shows an obvious hood of material attached to the core. Two stars shine through the tail.

Comet Halley	TYPE
FOV 15 min.	MAG 300 x

Comet Halley shot with Chris Schur's 135mm lens

Later we were lucky enough to photograph a "disconnection event." This means that a portion of the tail got released from the coma and moved off down the tail. The disconnected portion of the tail was above and to the right of the nucleus. In both photos, notice the rich Milky Way field of view. The comet was in the constellation of Norma, a part of the sky far to the south from the point of view of the continental United States or Europe.

With all this equipment, the naked eye view of the sky was still fascinating. The second brightest star, Canopus, was almost as bright as Sirius. Canopus was a little yellower and a little dimmer, but not much.

The comet showing the disconnected portion of the tail

The glow of the Milky Way paints the sky with stars from the Belt of Orion, through Sirius, to the False Cross in Vela, then on to Eta Carina, the Coal Sack, and then through Alpha and Beta Centauri. The False Cross has the same orientation and is a little larger than Crux, the real cross. There are several bright ovals along the Milky Way that are obvious open clusters. One is at the foot of the False Cross, and another is to the east of Eta Carina. The Eta Carina nebula reminds me of M6 or M7, a large and easily naked eye bright spot in Milky Way.

A wide-field image of the southern Milky Way. The dark Coal Sack is at the top, with Alpha and Beta Centauri below it. Scorpius is near the center, and the familiar rift in the Milky Way trails off over the horizon.

All too soon it was over. You know how time flies when you are having fun, and we were certainly having fun. The flight back seemed twice as long as the one to get over to Australia. But we did sleep quite a bit on the plane; there was lots of catching up to do.

I have been very fortunate to have several people in my life who have been friends of mine for over thirty years. David, Chris, and Jim and Lynn are high on that list. As I write this in 2010, David and I have plans to go out telescoping this weekend. And we have often said how we would like to return to Australia.

CHAPTER 5: JUNE 27, 1987

SEDONA: MAYNARD AND JEAN CLARK'S HOUSE

I believe anyone who does something that they love will have memories of places that produce that warm feeling of time well spent. For me, they seem to continually happen with people who enjoy viewing the sky and places that are located under dark skies far from city lights.

In the Saguaro Astronomy Club we were fortunate to have as members Maynard and Jean Clark. They lived in Sedona, a lively little hamlet about seventy-five miles north of Phoenix. Sedona is in the heart of the Red Rocks country in a beautiful location surrounded by very colorful geology. It was well worth the trip to view the sky during the night and then wake up surrounded by the beauty of nature.

Every year they would invite the club up to share a weekend at their place. The good news is they had enough land that we could all set up telescopes with some room left over. More good news is that their neighbors rarely turned on porch lights, so it was dark. It became a trip that the club members talked about and looked forward to attending for years.

The Saguaro Astronomy Club visiting the Clarks in Sedona

Sedona Red Rocks

As far as telescopes were concerned, my story left off with me owning a large but clumsy eighteen-inch Dobsonian. Even though there were terrific views to be had with that telescope, it had two major flaws. I already hit upon the fact that it was difficult to set up and tear down, and this really detracted from the joys of the telescope. The other problem is that it did not track the sky.

I found that I missed a "driven" telescope. My first scope, the eight-inch f/6, was small, but the motor and gear mechanism in the mount would track along with wherever you pointed it. This means that it would keep the Moon, planet, or galaxy in the field of view. Both of the large Dobsonian telescopes I built, the 17.5-inch and eighteen-inch scopes, would not track, so they had to be pushed along about every thirty seconds or so to keep the scope pointed at the correct location as the Earth rotated on its axis. If you are trying to make a drawing, this can be quite irritating. I realized that I wanted a tracking telescope that was larger than the old eight-incher.

Now enters Pierre Schwaar. Pierre had lived in Tucson for some time but decided to move to Phoenix. Boy, am I glad. Pierre was one of those rare folks who are both a telescope maker and an observer. Once I saw that he was grinding and polishing mirrors and then building a tracking mount to fit the scope, I was sold.

I was considering buying a new Toyota truck and needed to know the length of the bed. Picture the salesman finding me in the back of a new truck with a tape measure. He said, "What are you doing?" and I said, "Seeing if my telescope will fit." He immediately looked at me as if I were an escaped mental patient. But my credit was good and we quickly closed the deal.

The length of the bed of that truck determined the focal length of the telescope I had Pierre make for me. Focal length is the distance from the front of the mirror to the location of the eyepiece. The thirteen-inch (330mm) telescope Pierre made for me had a focal length of seventy-four inches (1880mm). Often the ratio of these two numbers is given as the "focal ratio" or "f/ratio." The number for my thirteen-inch scope was an f/5.6 telescope.

Today many telescope manufacturers are grinding mirrors to very short focal ratios, often around f/4 and less. I have found that these telescopes do not provide as sharp an image as my thirteen-inch, but you can look for yourself. Much of what an observer decides will work for them will not work for someone else. It is good that we have choices.

Once this telescope was built, I was happy. It was much larger than the eight-inch, so it will show many more objects and lots of detail within them. Also, it was driven with an electric motor and gear system. I owned the thirteen-inch scope for fourteen years, the longest of any telescope I have ever had. I viewed all the objects in *Burnham's Celestial Handbook* with this telescope. I had a friend who worked with me for years and then moved to a small Arizona town north of Prescott to teach high school. His school purchased the scope, and it is used by students there to this day. It is always pleasing to me to see a telescope wind up in the hands of someone who will make good use of it once I am ready to sell it.

Back to the Clarks' property and a beautiful night among the red rocks of northern Arizona. The seeing was rated at seven out of ten, and the transparency was eight out of ten, an excellent night for observing the sky.

Sedona using the thirteen-inch scope

Once the sun went down and the stars came out, I saw that Virgo was as high as it would be that night. There are lots of galaxies in the constellation of the Virgin, and M 104 had been one of my favorites for many years. This started me viewing a variety of Messier objects for the "first light" of the thirteen-inch. It turned out to be a very memorable evening indeed.

M 104 is a bright galaxy with a dark lane across it. Using the new thirteen-inch at 100X I saw it as large and very much elongated, about 4X1 elongated. It was suddenly much brighter in the middle, and the core "sat" on the northern edge of the dark lane. Raising the power to 150X provided a nice view; using averted vision doubled the size of the galaxy, both in length and width. There was a thirteenth magnitude star to the north side, centered above the core. At 220X there was some scalloped detail in the edges of the dark lane. The core area showed a small stellar nucleus about 20 percent of the time.

M 104

M 3 is a globular cluster in the constellation of Canes Venatici, the hunting dogs. On a good night this is certainly a *wow* object. Using 220X it was very bright, very large, and very suddenly much brighter in the middle. I counted ninety-two stars resolved within the cluster. The central small one arc minute of the core was the only portion not resolved. Going to 330X with a 6.7mm eyepiece, the core was now completely resolved.

Lord Rosse was an Irishman who built the world's largest telescope in 1848. It was a seventy-two-inch reflector. Using that telescope, Lord Rosse saw several dark markings in M 3. In the thirteen-inch they were evident to the north and south of the core, about three arc minutes on either side. They could be seen as small, thin dark lanes winding their way through a myriad of stars.

M 2

M 57 is the Ring Nebula in Lyra, the Lyre. It is a famous object because it is easy to locate, and it is easily the brightest nebula that looks like an annulus, or circular structure. At 60X the annular structure was seen, even at low power—it is the Ring Nebula all the time! Raising the power to 150X provided a great view. It was bright, large, and elongated 1.5X1. This nebula was a lovely greenish donut in a nice field rich with stars.

One hundred and fifty years ago John Herschel said that the center of the Ring was not dark; there is a faint glow within it. He described it as "gauze across a hoop." At 330X this effect was obvious. At this power and higher I could just catch a glimpse of the central star. It never held steady, but for just a moment it would flash at me.

A drawing of M 57, the Ring Nebula, with the thirteen-inch telescope at 330X. I drew the central star as there, even though it was only seen in short moments of good seeing.

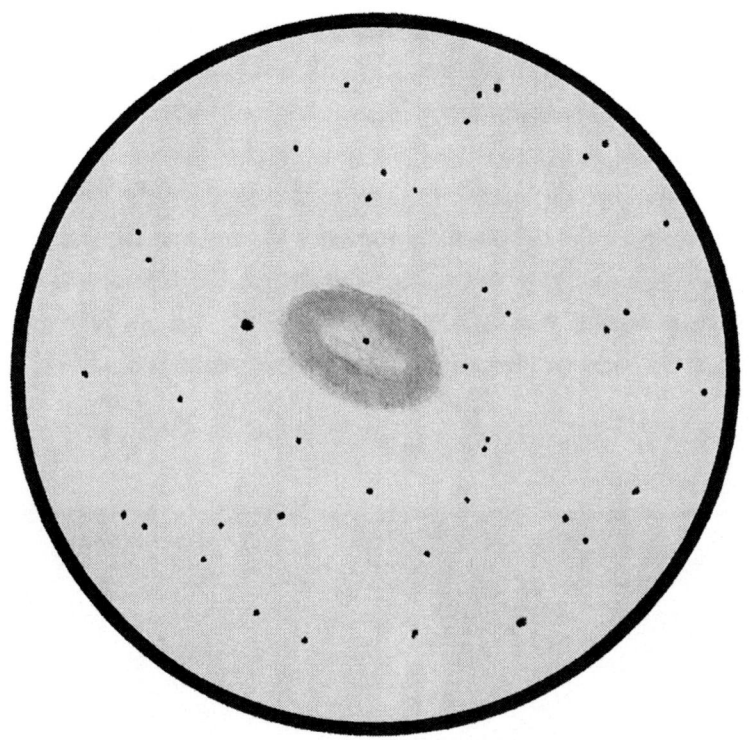

I decided to try M 20, the Trifid Nebula in Sagittarius, just to see how much detail the thirteen-inch scope would provide.

At 100X it was bright and large with an irregular shape, like a figure eight. There were thirty-eight stars involved; a very faint outer shell of nebulosity extended east and west from the main Trifid shape. The dark lanes that cut it into thirds and gave it that name were obvious; they extended out into the very faint outer nebulosity. Adding the UHC filter really showed off this nebula at its best. It looked just like a picture; the filter got rid of the faintest stars involved but provided a spectacular view of the nebula. Dark crooked lanes cut the nebula to pieces and divided the north blue and south red section.

I took the scope to 220X to see what I could see of the double star in the middle. This multiple star, HN 40, was discovered by William Herschel. The combination of a great telescope and a terrific night resolved this as actually a triple star. At this power, there was a twelfth-magnitude companion star to the north of the bright pair. At this power the nebula filled the field of view and the dark lanes cut through that glow with much fine detail. The central star of the northern section was light orange. The UHC did not help at this power; the view was better at higher powers without the filter.

M 20

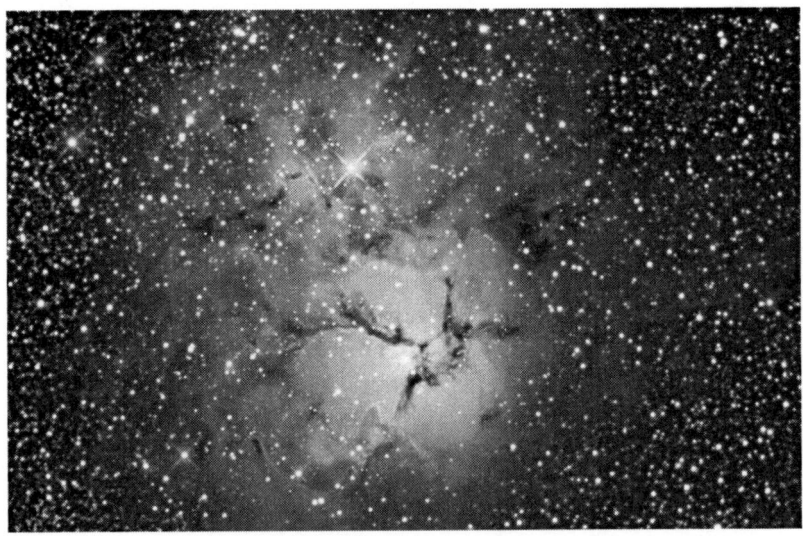

After a long night of observing the skies, we were always in for a treat. Jeannie Clark would fix breakfast for all the SAC members in attendance. It was the perfect end to a great time. You just don't realize how much moving that telescope around all night will build up an appetite.

Maynard and Jeannie Clark (right) at SAC holiday party; with the beard is Gene Lucas, an original SAC member.

Chapter 6: September 17, 1988

Lowell Observatory

Of all the planets beyond the orbit of Earth to observe, Mars is the most variable in size and detail. Jupiter, Saturn, Uranus, and Neptune all look pretty much the same size regardless of where the Earth is in its orbit. That is because they are very far away.

Mars really changes its size, which changes the amount of detail you can see, as it goes around in its orbit. When Mars is close to Earth it is large and will show lots of detail on its surface. When Mars is far away it is tiny, and this makes it difficult to see the features on its surface.

Therefore, an observer of Mars waits for those times when Mars is at "opposition." This is when it is opposite the Sun and therefore high in the sky at midnight. The complexities of Mars's orbit means that not all oppositions are the same—some are better than others. The year 1988 brought with it a very good opposition of Mars. It would be over twenty-three arc seconds in size. That is quite large for the Red Planet.

Let me digress and discuss angular size. There are three values used to measure angular size. Because the Babylonians used a "base sixty" number system for this, the three measurements are multiples of sixty one from the other, just like there are sixty minutes in an hour of time.

The largest measure is an arc degree. One degree is one 360th of a circle. The Pleiades, the bright star cluster in Taurus, is almost two degrees in size. The distance between the pointer stars in the Big Dipper is about five degrees, and the full Moon is about half of one degree.

One sixtieth of one degree is one arc minute. The Ring Nebula is a little larger than one arc minute in size. Many Messier open clusters are between twenty and thirty arc minutes in size. Alberio, the beautiful double star in Cygnus, has a distance between the two stars of just under one arc minute.

One sixtieth of one arc minute is one arc second. Jupiter is about forty arc seconds in size. The distance between many multiple stars is measured in arc seconds. If you have a night of very good seeing you will be able to use high power and split double stars of one arc second. That is rare in central Arizona; the movement of the atmosphere will rarely allow the seeing to be that good. As I said, Mars on the night we are discussing was twenty-three arc seconds in size. That is large for Mars, and we were hoping to see lots of detail on the disk of the Red Planet.

I am fortunate to have as a friend Brian Skiff. He has worked at Lowell Observatory for many years and has helped with a wide variety of observing projects. He was nice enough to invite several SAC members to Lowell to view Mars during this excellent opposition. We jumped at the chance.

The twenty-four-inch Clark refractor at Lowell Observatory has been on Mars Hill in Flagstaff for over one hundred years as I write this. Refractors use lenses to bring light to focus. All the telescopes I have been discussing up to now are reflectors, which use a mirror.

The twenty-four-inch refractor at Lowell has a twenty-four-inch pair of lenses at the top of the long tube. These carefully polished lenses were made by the famous Clark family in Massachusetts.

The Clark refractor at the Lowell Observatory

These old refractors are from an era long gone. Over one hundred years ago when this telescope was made, it was very difficult to make a refractor with a short focal length and to test the curved figure of the glass. To get the views nice and sharp, these telescopes were made very long, very long indeed.

The twenty-four-inch refractor at Lowell Observatory is an f/15 telescope. This means that the tube is twenty-four inches times fifteen inches long. That is thirty feet (ten meters) from the glass objective at the top down to the observer at the bottom. In the nineteenth century, when you purchased a big telescope, you got a big telescope, in all directions.

Percival Lowell of Boston had the money and the time to take on astronomy with lots of vigor and became a celebrity in the early twentieth century, when he believed he was seeing canals on Mars. Lowell thought that the clear air in Arizona was allowing him to see detail on Mars that few others saw. These dark lines across the face of Mars were supposed by him to be a giant canal project to move water from the poles of Mars down to the deserts at the equator. Lowell saw hundreds of canals and believed until his death that he was seeing a civilization at work on a giant project to try to save itself. Of course, once we sent spacecraft cameras to Mars, we saw that the canals were an optical illusion.

We arrived in the afternoon, and Brian was nice enough to open up the telescope for us to examine. We were like kids in a candy factory. AJ and I took photos of everything we saw and enjoyed listening to stories about how the scope had been erected when Flagstaff, Arizona, was a frontier logging community.

Examining the observer's end of the big refractor

From right to left: Jerry Maurer, AJ Crayon, me (kneeling), Curt Taylor, Brian Skiff, Bob Erdman, George DeLange

AJ trying to move the twenty-four-inch refractor. I told you it was big and heavy.

After an afternoon of fun examining the telescope, we left the dome so that Brian could give a public viewing session. Our group adjourned to the parking lot, and Curt Taylor set up his four-inch Quantum telescope so we could view for a while. AJ and I pulled out our binoculars for some Milky Way viewing.

We spent some time on the crescent Moon and the Sea of Serenity, which has some fascinating cracks along the floor. The craters Eudoxus and Aristotelles are also near the terminator. Aristotelles showed an ejecta blanket of material that was thrown out when the impact crater was formed. There were terraced walls and an obvious central peak at 175X in the four-inch scope.

We also spent some time with Saturn before it passed in among the pine trees. I have never tired of that amazing ball within a ring. The planet Uranus was about 1½ degrees to the southeast of Saturn. However, it is small enough that it was only a tiny greenish disk at 175X.

AJ and I were having a lot of fun with the binoculars, and we passed them around to others in the group. We were looking at many of the showpieces along the Milky Way before they got into the trees. After all these years of viewing the sky, I have never tired of a good view of the Milky Way in binoculars. Also, they are easily the handiest viewing device one can use.

Once public viewing was over we moved into the dome of the twenty-four-inch Clark refractor. Brian had mentioned that the eyepieces were rather old and not nearly as good as modern eyepieces, so I had brought my eyepiece box and we set it near the pier of the scope and were ready for the night.

Brian said that the views were better with the telescope "stopped down" to eighteen inches. There was a metal iris at the top of the tube that had a long rod down to the observer. This rod and handle allowed the user to make the aperture of the telescope smaller. Brian said that for the planets the views were better because the smaller aperture sharpens the view. We believed him.

On this particular night, Mars was 23.7 arc seconds in size and the south polar cap was facing the Earth. This white area of ice was easily seen as the most prominent feature. There were some dark markings seen; the Eye of Mars (Solis Lacus) was the easiest to see of the dark areas. All of this was at 455X with no filters.

Solis Lacus (the Eye of Mars) is the obvious feature near the top of Mars at 455X in my drawing. The polar cap is at the bottom.

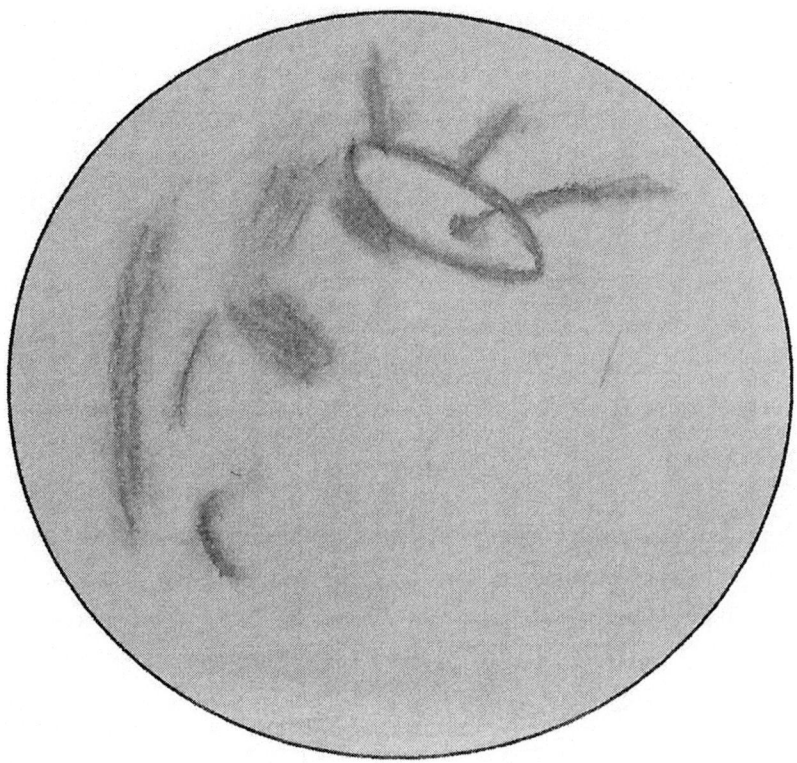

Mars is the "Red Planet" because the dust and rocks across its face contain iron oxide. This is the same mineral that is also called "rust" when it attacks ferrous metal. I find it fascinating that the rocks at the Grand Canyon, Sedona, and southern Utah are all the same chemical composition as the reddish disk I am observing.

We were using the same telescope that Percival Lowell used to see hundreds of canals and other very fine details across its face. We added a light red filter to bring out the dark markings, and sure enough in moments of steady viewing I would see several faint lines superimposed onto Mars. I will not say that I saw canals because there were only four or five lines that I am discussing, but they were there.

The other side of this mystery is that Lowell drew straight-line features on Venus and Mercury as well as Mars. Maybe they were just a feature of his eye and brain straining to see the most difficult detail.

Later on we moved to Jupiter and got a truly "wow" view. This giant planet is divided up by bands that include light ovals, dark "barges," and most famously, the Great Red Spot. All of these were available on this night at 455X with no filter. It was a wonderful view of one of my favorites in the sky.

Jupiter is easily the largest planet; the rest of the planets in the solar system would fit inside it. I really enjoy watching the detail across the disk of Jupiter change. The "festoons" are curved markings that seem to rise up out of one band and fade out. They look like a saber-toothed tiger's fangs to me. All in all, there is plenty to see on Jupiter.

Being the deep-sky crazies that we are, we insisted on viewing something beyond the solar system before the end of this terrific night, so we looked at M 15, an excellent globular cluster in Pegasus. It was an explosion of stars, with color. It is rare to see color in a globular cluster, but with the big refractor there were white, yellow, light-orange, and a few very light-blue stars in the field.

My drawing of Jupiter at 455X with the twenty-four-inch stopped down to eighteen inches of aperture

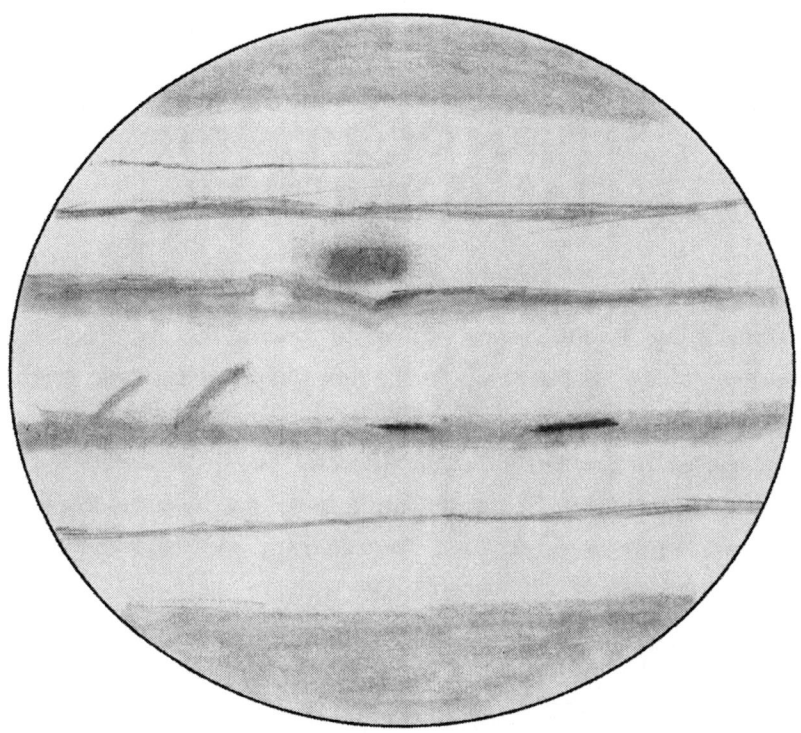

I knew this was going to be a memorable night before we started. First we had a chance to look over one of the most famous telescopes in the world. This was followed by a fun observing session in the parking lot before viewing with the Clark refractor. Then there was a night with clear skies and good seeing so that we could see plenty of detail on the planets. This was what the twenty-four-inch refractor was built to provide. We all went away with great memories.

Chapter 7: July 2, 1989

⸺ℳ⸺

Saturn Occults the Star 28 Sagitarrii

Many things happen repeatedly while viewing the sky. The Sun, Moon, planets, and stars rise in the east and set in the west. As the seasons change the point along the horizon where the Sun rises or sets moves. In the northern hemisphere as the Sun is further to the south, winter arrives. When the Sun is to the north, summer is here and it is hot in central Arizona. You can count on those happenings as a regular event.

There are other things going on in the sky that are rare. We will get to several of these as the book progresses: bright comets, meteor storms, and total solar eclipses. This chapter will cover another rare event, a planetary occultation of a star. This means that a planet passes in front of a star and occults, or blocks off, the star's light for a short period of time. As I write this I am sixty-one years old, and only two of these events have happened in my lifetime. Far and away the most interesting is the occultation of the star 28 Sagitarrii by the ringed planet Saturn.

AJ Crayon and I planned to observe this event from somewhere in central Arizona. The weather and cloud cover would allow us to make the final decision about which way to drive for this occultation. It turned out that the southern part of the state was covered in clouds, so we decided to drive north. We went to an observing site we had used many times before, Dugas Road. It is near the city of Prescott and about sixty miles from Phoenix.

I packed up the scope into my Toyota truck and drove over to AJ's house and we got going. AJ and I chatted on the CB radio while driving along, which passed the time nicely. One of the things we talked about was whether the rings would be thick enough to completely block off the star. The rings of Saturn are made up of many trillions of pieces of ice and some rocky rubble with gaps. It would be fun to see what happens as the rings move in front of the star.

AJ was going to use his trusty eight-inch f/6 Newtonian. If anyone has ever gotten more out of one telescope they are a rare observer. Many of my friends use a variety of telescopes over the years, but AJ is the exception. He had had the eight-incher for nine years at the time of this occultation and would keep on using this scope for another eleven years for a total of twenty years of use. When he finally decided to sell it he had certainly gotten all he was going to get out that telescope.

AJ with the eight-inch Newtonian

75

I will be using the thirteen-inch Newtonian that I discussed in the chapter about Sedona.

The thirteen-inch Newtonian scope and me
at the Dugas Road observing site

It was a Sunday evening and was New Moon. We had not gone out for a New Moon weekend observing session because of the clouds. Because of all this, there were only the two of us to see this rare event. We got there at sunset and had a sandwich in twilight hoping for the clouds to stay away. Because the occultation would not start for several hours after dark, I did some observing in the constellation of Ophiuchus, the Snake Handler.

Rho Ophiuchi is a multiple star with four components. Two of the stars are a wide split; they are over two arc minutes from the primary and could be seen in the finder scope. The primary pair is fifth and sixth magnitude divided by three arc seconds. I could get a clean split at 135X. The primary was yellow, and the three companions were light blue. A gorgeous combination!

NGC 6572 is a planetary nebula. These nebulae are the remnants of stars like the Sun. They puff off the outer layers of their atmosphere and the hot core is left behind to illuminate the nebula. This one was bright, large, and elongated 1.5X1 using 220X in the thirteen-inch. The central star was held steady in good seeing conditions. At other times the center would just brighten up somewhat. The noteworthy aspect of this gem was its color. In every scope I have ever owned, from an eight-inch to an eighteen-inch, this is the greenest nebula I have ever seen! The ionized oxygen in this gas cloud make the nebula as green as an Irishman's coat on St. Patrick's Day. All right, it is as green as Key lime pie.

NGC 6572

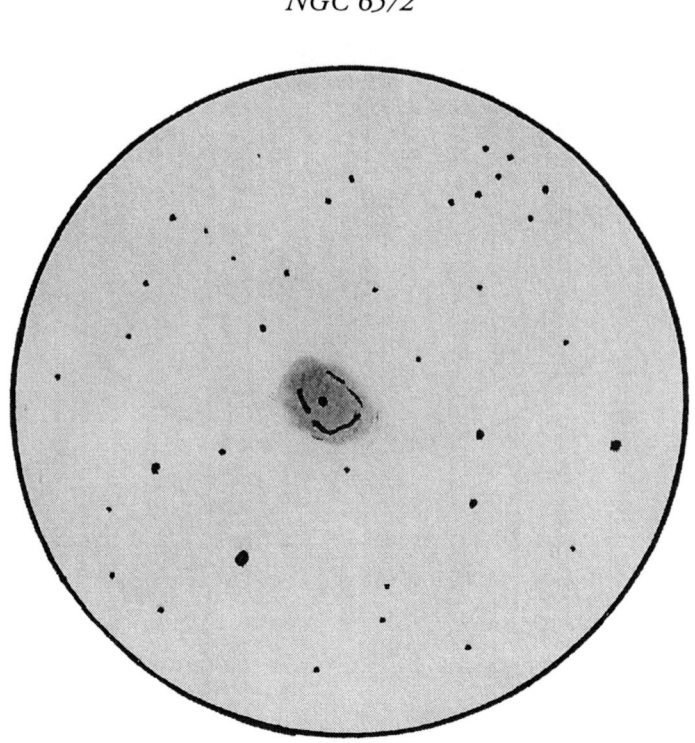

NGC 6633 is an open cluster. At 60X it was bright, large, and little compressed. This pretty rich cluster showed several nice chains of stars. I counted thirty-two stars involved within the cluster. Several stars showed color; there were two blue and three yellow stars in this cluster.

NGC 6633

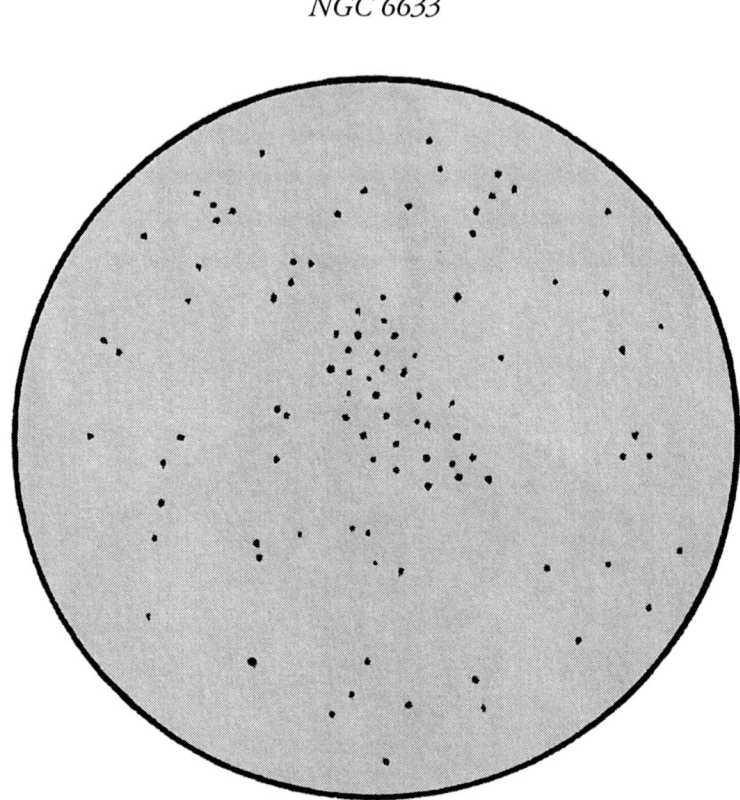

From the previous observations, I rated the seeing at five out of ten. That is mediocre, but like most nights, if you stay at the eyepiece and really observe there will be moments of better seeing that will allow you see more detail. By now the occultation was starting; let the show begin:

All the times are Mountain Standard Time (Arizona does not change to Daylight Savings Time).

11:15 PM: The star 28 Sagitarrii is at the edge of the rings of Saturn, and the action starts. The rings of Saturn have been given letters to designate their position, with the "A" ring being outside and the "C" ring being inside.

As AJ and I watched, the star winked on and off within the "A" ring. There was enough material to completely block off the star, but just barely in the A ring. Between the A and B rings is the Cassini division. This is named after an astronomer who was first able to spot this most obvious gap in the rings.

11:28 PM: The star is in the Cassini division. This is the most interesting view in my opinion. The star returns to its original magnitude before encountering the rings. The star is silvery white and the rings are ivory; the contrast between the two is striking.

An image of the star 28 Sagitarrii in the Cassini division using the planetarium program Sky Map Pro 11. Thank you to Chris Mariott.

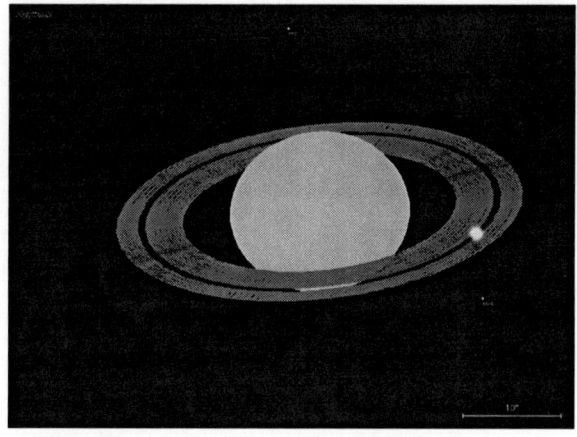

Now the star dives into the wider "B" ring and disappears until it emerges into the "crepe ring" or "C" ring. Within the wispy crepe ring it flickers for two minutes until it returns to full brightness between Saturn and the inside of the rings.

11:50 PM: The star is at the edge of the ball of Saturn itself and starts to fade into the gaseous atmosphere of Saturn. The star takes on a light orange hue as it moves into the atmosphere. I count off "one thousand one, one thousand two ..." until the star disappears completely from view. The total time for that to happen is fifteen seconds by my very unscientific method. And it is over.

*Another image from Sky Map Pro as the star
enters the atmosphere of Saturn*

AJ and I took a deep breath and looked up from the eyepiece. The entire enthralling event only took forty-five minutes, but it was worth all the effort to observe it. Terrestrial clouds were starting to thicken up in the south, and we realized that we are not going to view the reemergence of the star from the other side of Saturn. We tore down the telescopes, talking all the time about what an amazing view it was and wondering if there would be another anytime soon. The answer to that question was no. Besides, it was Sunday night at midnight and we had to get to work the next day to pay for all the gasoline we had burned up.

CHAPTER 8: MARCH 9, 1991

BUCKEYE PARK: OBSERVING HERSCHEL 400

I want to take one chapter of this book and discuss what happens on a "regular" night out with the telescope. On this evening we were at a site about sixty miles (one hundred kilometers) from the lights of Phoenix at a spot we called "Buckeye" in the Buckeye Hills Recreation Area, near the little town of Buckeye, Arizona. Obviously, someone who moved here was from Ohio.

Even though a drive of over ninety miles was needed to really get the lights of Phoenix to shrink down to a small light dome, sometimes you just can't, or don't want to, drive that far to observe. Much of this depended on the phase of the Moon. If the Moon was rising around midnight, then we would generally do a "one nighter." That means to drive out to the site, set the scopes, observe until moonrise, and then return home. Only on New Moon or near to it would the club do a "two nighter" and drive to the site on Friday after work and then observe for two nights and return on Sunday. A two nighter made it worthwhile to drive further from the city.

At this time I was observing the objects in the Herschel 400 list from the Astronomical League. It contained their choices for the best four hundred objects that were cataloged by William Herschel early in the nineteenth century. He had been a hero of mine for many years, a man who saw what he wanted to do and was tough minded about doing it. William Herschel decided to scan the entire sky available to him and look for clusters and nebulae. Eventually, he published three lists that added up to 2,500 discoveries, an amazing feat in the era of visual observing.

Herschel used a big, clumsy telescope, and so he decided to just use the rotation of the Earth to move the scope along a straight line and see what came into the field of view. This was an efficient but time-consuming task. But obviously it worked.

Herschel's telescope on display at the Smithsonian Air and Space Museum in Washington, DC, showing a mockup of William at the eyepiece as he speaks his observations to his sister, Caroline, in the second-story window.

The handles on the twenty-foot telescope at the Smithsonian Air and Space Museum in Washington, DC. When the guards were not looking I reached over and touched the handles that were used to control the altitude of the tube. Please don't turn me in.

Okay, back to Buckeye and a night of observing. Along with me and the thirteen-inch scope were Tom Polakis, Rich Walker, and Pierre Schwaar, the manufacturer of my telescope. On a night like this, I generally made an observing list so I could keep track of what I observed and how close I was to the end of my task.

I understand that for some people this "takes the fun out of observing," and for them that is the truth. I have many observing buddies who take no notes of any type, and that is their choice. I would like to say that for me having notes and drawings adds so much to my experience of viewing the sky that I must at least try to get you to see my point of view.

Now that I am officially "too old to die young," these notes and observations bring me a real sense of joy. I enjoy reading my old observations and viewing those drawings because they allow me to relive what I saw on that evening. I generally also write down who else was observing with me that night and where we were set up. Once you take the time to get good at it, taking a note about what is in the eyepiece only takes a few minutes and is worth it, I promise. Make yourself get started, and before you know it you will have a library that will serve as a memory aid for years to come.

Below is my observing list for the night. In order, the data given is NGC number, Constellation, Object Type, Right Ascension, Declination, Magnitude, Size and Herschel Number.

Here is an explanation of some of that information. The NGC is New General Catalog, released in 1888 and based on Herschel's work; it is a good catalog of the brightest objects in the sky. CON is the constellation in which this object is located, all Puppis for this list. Type is the object type—open cluster, galaxy, globular cluster, and planetary nebula. RA and DEC are the celestial latitude and longitude that tell you where in the sky this object is located. Size is given in arc minutes (') and arc seconds ("), so the two planetary nebulae are smaller than the open clusters on the list. The Herschel numbers are the designations provided by Herschel's original list.

NGC	Con	TYPE	RA	DEC	Mag	Size	H numb
2423	PUP	OPNCL 07	37.1	-13 52	6.7	19.0'	H VII 28
2438	PUP	PLNNB 07	41.8	-14 44	11.0	65"	H IV 39
2440	PUP	PLNNB 07	41.9	-18 13	11.5	54"X20"	H IV 64
2489	PUP	OPNCL 07	56.2	-30 04	7.9	8.0'	H VII 23
2539	PUP	OPNCL 08	10.7	-12 50	6.5	22.0'	H VII 11

With all that in mind, let's see what was observed on the night of March 9, 1991, with the thirteen-inch telescope.

NGC 2423 was large, pretty bright, pretty rich, and pretty compressed, and thirty-three stars were counted at 100X. There was a nice binary star in the center with both components a lovely dark yellow.

NGC 2438 was bright, large, and elongated 1.2X1 in position angle seventy-five degrees. The central star was easy at 100X. Raising the power to 440X brought out two dimmer stars involved in the nebula. Also at the higher power the shape of the planetary was seen to be an incomplete ring, somewhat like a horseshoe. This bright rim was about 270 degrees around and was dimmest on the north side. I had always seen this planetary nebula as light green in color. This planetary was at the edge of the cluster Messier 46.

NGC 2438

A drawing I made of NGC 2438 at 330X

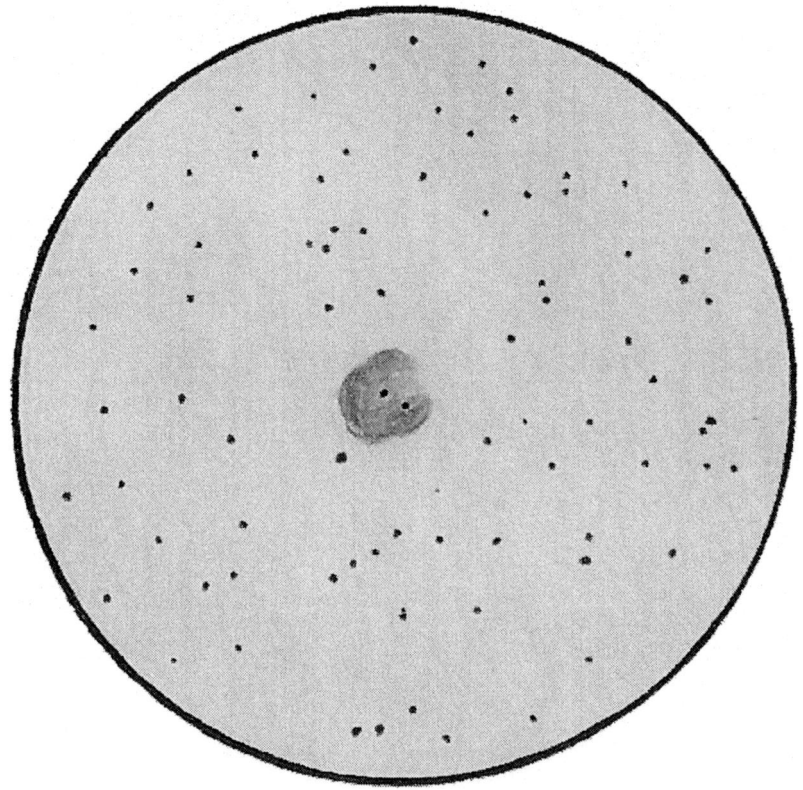

NGC 2440 is another planetary nebula. It could be easily seen as non-stellar at 100X. At 270X it was bright, pretty large, much brighter in the middle, and elongated 2X1 in PA 30. The central star becomes stellar in moments of good seeing, but most of the time it was just a bright area in the center of this planetary. Averted vision about doubles the size of the nebula. This nebula showed a nice lime green at all powers.

A drawing of NGC 2440 made at 270X

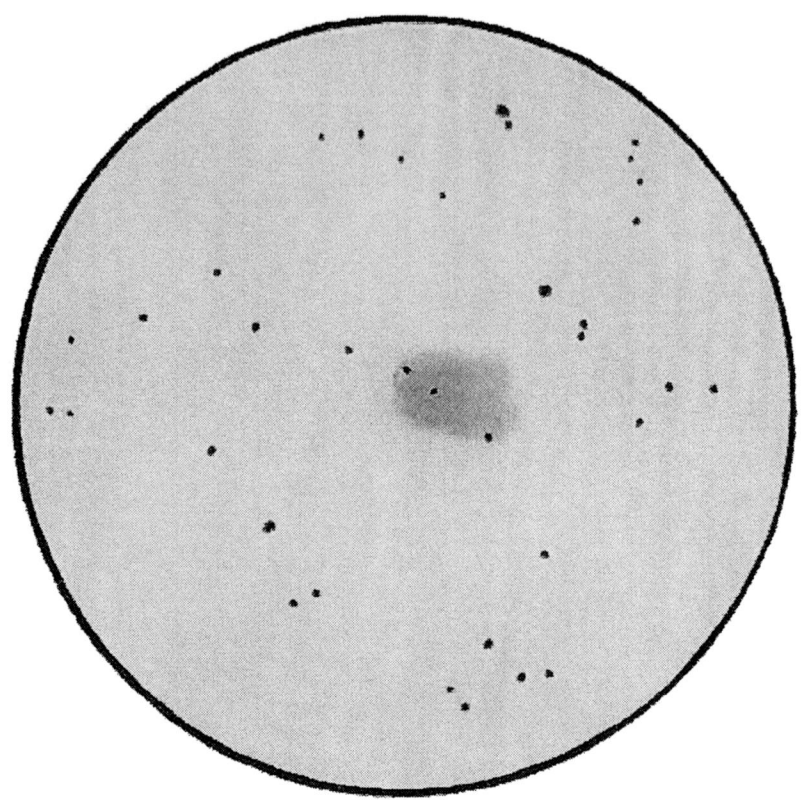

NGC 2489 was bright enough to see in the 11X80 finder scope. At 100X it was bright, pretty large, pretty rich, and not compressed. I counted thirty-one stars involved within the cluster, some in nice curving chains of stars. This cluster was moderately well detached from the background glow of the Puppis Milky Way.

A drawing of NGC 2489 made at 100X

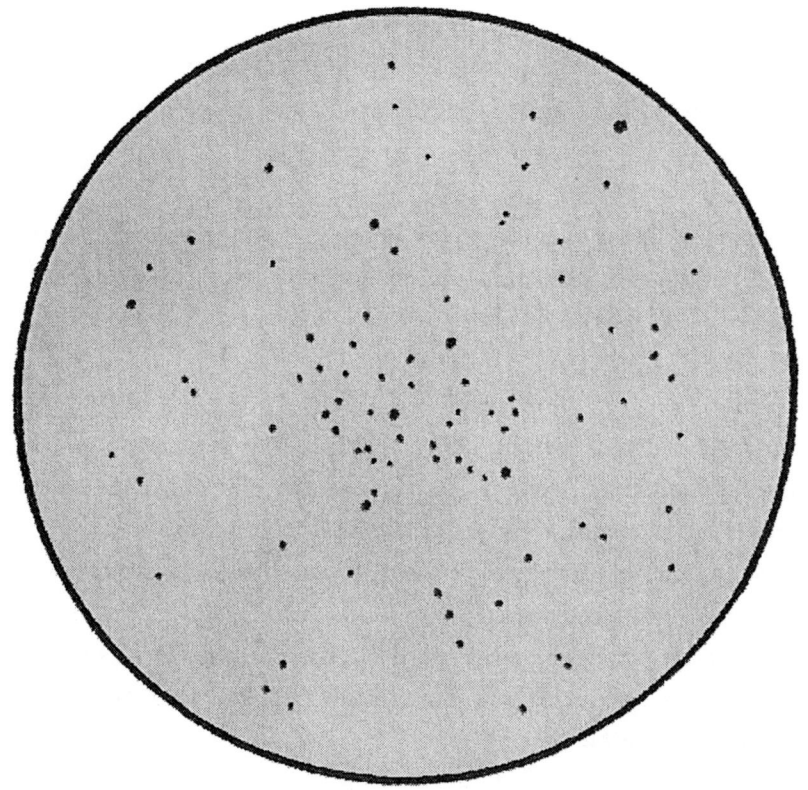

NGC 2539 was located on the south side of the star 19 Puppis, and I first saw it as a faint glow in the 10X50 binoculars as I was star-hopping to its position. At 100X it was bright, large, rich, and elongated 2X1. I counted sixty-five stars of magnitudes ten to thirteen involved within the cluster. This little compressed cluster had a double star of tenth magnitude just to the west. Star 19 PUP was on the south side of this cluster. It was a wide triple star, easy to split at 100X; the stars were a yellow primary with two white companions.

Yes, there are some objects that look similar to others, but no two are absolutely identical. Writing down a set of notes that provide evidence for what you have seen will help you picture differences in these objects. If you don't really observe, you are just glancing at what is in the eyepiece. Spend some time, relax, and enjoy the view.

One of the things I found early in my note-taking career was that for really bright and spectacular objects my notes consisted of essentially "wow." Or, maybe "wowee." Not a very useful observation, I admit.

So I created the "Bright Objects Project" to get myself to start writing more than "wow." I set up an observing list of Messier objects and the Best of the NGC from the SAC website. Each of the 220 objects got one full page of printout. For each object I had to fill the page with my handwritten notes while at the eyepiece under dark skies. It does make you write more, but these famous objects deserve to be written about. If you must fill up the page, this process also makes you print larger;-).

I was happy once I completed the Herschel 400 list. It is a good list and keeps the name of my hero in the minds of people observing the night sky. I am writing this in my motor home, and my H 400 certificate is hanging on the wall. Go to the Astronomical League website and download the list. Once you are done, you will be a proud deep-sky observer, I promise.

CHAPTER 9: JUNE 18, 1993

✐

GRAND CANYON NORTH

My astronomy buddies and I observed for many years from locations that were about a two-hour drive from Phoenix. We had lots of great observations from those places and enjoyed them very much. One thing about people in general is that they often seem to wonder about what is just over the next hill. We started to wonder what a trip much further from the lights of Phoenix would provide, so we began to plan a long trip to the North Rim of the Grand Canyon. This is about a five-hour drive, and we would be at about nine-thousand-feet altitude. Ah, if we only knew what we were getting into.

As we chatted among ourselves about this trip, we set some limitations. First, the weather would have to be perfect; there would be no prospect of being clouded out. Second, if we were going to invest the time and money to do this, it would be only on a New Moon weekend. We would have to maximize the dark observing time, so there will be no Moon in the sky. Third, it has to be either before or after the "monsoons" in Arizona. There is a weather joke in the Southwestern United States that the "rainy season" of the summer is called the monsoons. We get about five inches of rain during this time, probably 1 percent of a proper Asian monsoon.

The limiting conditions all were met in June of 1993, and we decided to take on the long trip to view the sky from the North Rim.

Everything got packed up, and I double-checked my list of what to take. It is very aggravating to get to a distant observing site only to find that you left something vital behind.

While driving up Interstate 17 toward Flagstaff we talked on the CB radio about what we were planning to view and how much fun this was going to be. We stopped and got a delicious cheeseburger in Flagstaff and continued on our way north.

It is amazing how friendship can change your time enjoying a hobby. Few people have one friend who is part of their life for as long I have known these three friends. As I write this we have been going out observing together for thirty years. I don't ever remember an angry word among us. We have spent many hours viewing the sky together. I met all three at an astronomy club. If you have a club near you, then make the time to attend some meetings and encourage others to join in the fun. It can enrich your life.

The group on our way to the North Rim of the Grand Canyon. Right to left: me, AJ Crayon, David Fredericksen, and Bill Anderson

Having Bill Anderson along was a real joy. Bill taught geology at Phoenix College for many years and was able to point out to us a wide variety of rock formations and how they took on those amazing shapes and colors. It really passed the time listening to Bill inform the group about what we were seeing out the window.

The Vermillion Cliffs

At the little town of Jacob's Lake we stopped for several bags of ice and some local knowledge. One thing to know about the northern third of Arizona is that it is covered in pine trees. With that in mind we needed to find an opening that would let us view the sky, or at least a large part of it. The clerk at the store did not know of a place without trees.

So we decided to look for ourselves. Once we got about ten miles from Jacob's Lake we started taking turnoff roads to see what we could find. This is also where the CB radios came in handy. In an era before cell phones, being able to break into two groups and still talk to each other over a distance of three or four miles was very handy. In an hour or so we had found a spot that provided a view of much of the sky. The trees covered all the area really near the horizon, but there was plenty to view above the tree line.

The vehicles got parked, and we started to set up the telescopes. At this point the effects of being at 9,000 feet above sea level became obvious. There is a lot less oxygen here than we are used to at 1,500 feet in Phoenix. You would lift a counterweight, carry it ten feet, set it down, and then pant like a dog for three minutes. After breathing like you just ran in an Olympic event for a while you get enough strength to lift the next item you need to assemble the telescope. I am certainly happy we left early.

The scopes all set up at the observing site. Bill Anderson is on the left, standing, and David Fredericksen is on the right, seated.

After getting tired out setting up the scopes it was time for a simple meal, soup and a sandwich. As we sat down to eat and the Sun set, that glorious Arizona twilight started. Above the sunset was every color of the rainbow, and as time went on those colors got more subtle. If you turned around you could see the dark arc of the shadow of the Earth above the eastern horizon. All of this mixed in along the tree line in this beautiful setting.

As the brightest stars start to show themselves, we saw that Jupiter was near Spica, the brightest star in Virgo, so we got started observing some detail on Jupiter and exchanging views among the telescopes. As we were going at this, it was getting chilly. I slipped on my "moon boots" and an insulated suit in an effort to keep warm. As I was getting more layers on I made certain to add some thick socks and a wool cap. Every layer helps.

The Milky Way was coming out now, and my targets were within the constellation of Aquila, the Eagle, which is right along the Milky Way. That beautiful glow across the sky is the galaxy we live in. It is an edgewise disk of billions of stars, nebulae, and clusters.

I got out my star charts and started to look for NGC 6709, a cluster in Aquila. This open cluster was seen in the 11X80 finder. At 100X in the thirteen-inch scope I saw it as large, pretty rich, and not compressed. With about one minute's effort, fifty-nine members were counted. There were several nice chains of stars with a wide blue and gold double star on the western edge of the cluster. The cluster stood out well from the glow of the Milky Way.

Now I moved on to NGC 6804, a planetary nebula. At 135X it was pretty bright, pretty large, and round. Moving up to 220X showed four stars involved, including a twelfth-magnitude star on the eastern edge. Averted vision elongated the nebula; the pretty bright star involved also made the nebula appear comet shaped. It was round with direct vision. Adding the UHC filter showed the nebula with much better contrast.

My drawing of NGC 6804 at 220X in the thirteen-inch with no filter

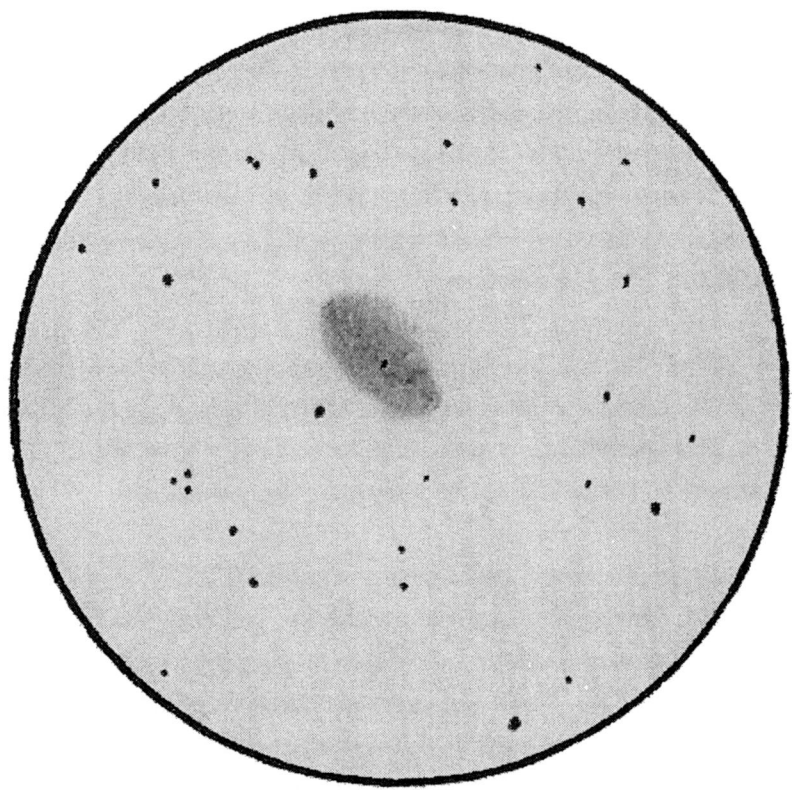

If you are going to chase a variety of nebulae, then several filters will help you see more detail. The wide-spectrum filter, or deep-sky filter, is better at blocking off light pollution for star clusters and galaxies. The effect of these types of filters is quite subtle.

The filter I would recommend for a novice is the narrow-band filter. The brand name from the Lumicon company is "UHC" for ultra-high contrast. These let through only the light associated with nebulae and block off much of the light from city street lights. They show the most detail in the most objects. I use mine often.

The most severe filters are the band-pass filters. The most common of these is the O III filter. Oxygen 3 is a very special type of oxygen ion that forms in nebulae. These filters let through only light from that special ion and nothing else. This means that you will need a telescope larger than six inches to see the real effect of these filters. They are getting rid of lots of the light from the nebulae. There are several other narrow-band filters, but most are created for astrophotography.

Back to enjoying our night of observing: We had a really fine evening, cool but bearable and certainly far from the city lights. I did notice one thing. Because we were somewhat oxygen-starved at this altitude, the sky was not dark. It was a medium grey and had texture somewhat like a huge quilt or rug. I never felt that I was seeing as much detail as I saw at lower altitudes. I also thought that by the next night it would be better. We would acclimatize to being at this altitude.

I did three other objects in Aquila. Barnard 142 and 143 are right next to each other and they are both dark nebulae. These dark markings along the Milky Way are large clouds of carbon, much like pencil lead. They block off the stars on the other side and so appear as dark because of the contrast with the background of Milky Way stars.

B 142 and 143 are 1 ½ degrees from Altair, the brightest star in Aquila. Because they appear like the capitol letter "E," they are often called the "E nebula." The dark nebulae were seen immediately in the 11X80 finder, so they were prominent under dark skies. In the thirteen-inch at 220X, there were no stars in an area about five by ten arc minutes in size. That is extraordinary. The "E" shape was easy to see with the 35mm Panoptic eyepiece. These large, dark fingers protrude out into a rich Milky Way field—a fascinating field of view.

An image of B 142 and 143 with an 85mm lens and my Canon DSLR camera. The bright star to the left is Altair, and the dark "E" feature faces right.

One last object in Aquila is the carbon star V Aquilae. Carbon stars are stars that have a cloud of carbon surrounding them. The carbon, literally soot, blocks off the blue light from the star, and so only red and orange light gets through this sooty cloud filter. It means that these carbon stars are the reddest stars in the sky, and

V Aquilae certainly proves that. At 100X in the thirteen-inch I saw it as burnt orange; several others in the group agree. If you are looking for something different from the usual observing fare, try carbon stars.

This night was one of those where I got to thinking about how unusual is the universe in which we live. Here is the chemical element carbon doing two completely different things. In a dark nebula it blocks off the light from distant stars, in some places completely. This effect can make a telescope located at a very dark viewing site see no stars through the thickest part of the dark nebula. Also, in carbon stars, this cloud of carbonaceous soot filters out blue and allows through red and orange, making the carbon star appear red or at least orange to my eye.

As the night progressed, the load of driving all day got to me, and by 2:00 AM I was tired out. I had one last look at Saturn and enjoyed that magnificent planet for a few minutes before climbing into the sleeping bag and dropping off with visions of the universe dancing in my head.

The next day we sat about for some time and discussed what we had seen and how much fun this weekend was already. A ranger stopped by to see how we were doing and told us that we had found one of the few open places around and that all the other open spots he knew were right on the edge of the Grand Canyon. We decided we had made a great decision setting up at this location. Having one of us go for a headlong dive into the Grand Canyon would rather take the edge off the fun.

On the next night I did a few objects in Ophiuchus. At 135X, M 62 was a very nice globular cluster that was not symmetrical. It was bright, large, elongated, and much brighter in the middle. This bizarre cluster has strings or chains of stars located on just one side of the globular. Therefore it appears to have a "beard" of stars trailing away to one side. Using 220X I could resolve twenty-eight stars in the cluster. I saw it as elongated 1.5X1 in PA 60 degrees, and there was a bright area that was offset to the southeast that may add to this appearance of elongation. Several chains of stars made their way out from core to the northwest. Averted vision made it grow a lot in all directions.

A drawing of M 62 at 220X

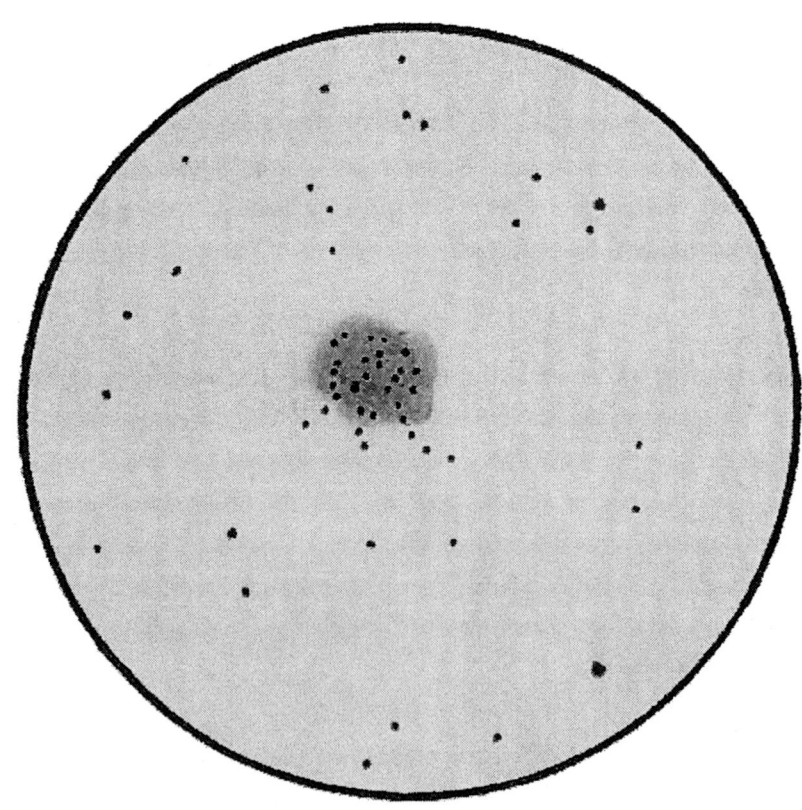

After I took on a few more famous and bright objects all around the sky I decided to pick up the 10X50 binoculars and see what I could see. I could just sit in a comfy chair and enjoy the view. It did seem that the sky was darker after getting used to being at high altitude. One of the best objects for this type of observing is the "Dark Horse" in Ophiuchus.

Richard Berry was the editor of *Astronomy Magazine* for many years, and he often attended the Riverside Telescope Makers Conference. One year he pointed out to me a dark marking in the sky that covered a very large area and looked, with just the naked eye, like a prancing horse. Sure enough, once you see it you can't miss it from a dark site.

An image of the "Dark Horse" with an 85mm lens and Canon DSLR camera. The "Pipe Nebula" is on the left with the stem of the pipe being the rear leg of the horse. On the bottom near center are the front legs; one leg is prancing. The head of the horse is less prominent and is right center. The "S" nebula is small and almost exactly centered.

Using the binoculars around the Dark Horse is also fascinating. There are bright and dark areas all around southern Ophiuchus, and the binoculars will bring out the detail and contrast that they can provide. Don't miss a binocular cruise in this part of the sky.

All too soon it was Sunday morning and we had to tear down the telescopes and drive back home. Again, we chatted on the CB radios about what we had seen and how great the skies were this far from the lights of civilization. The good news is that you see a lot more; the bad news is that you realize how much the encroachment of city lights is reducing what can be observed close to town.

Chapter 10: July 18, 1994

Jupiter Struck by Comet SL9

About a year before the observations in this chapter, Gene and Carolyn Shoemaker along with David Levy used the eighteen-inch Schmidt camera at Mount Palomar to discover a most unusual comet. Carolyn described it as a "squashed" comet from its appearance on the discovery photograph. It turned out that the comet had passed very close to Jupiter and the powerful gravity of the largest planet had torn the comet to pieces. An image from the Hubble Space Telescope showed a "string of pearls" as the pieces of the comet stretched out from the force of Jupiter's gravity.

After some orbit calculations were made it was realized that in the middle of July 1994 this object, now called Comet Shoemaker-Levy 9 (SL9), would impact the planet Jupiter. At the time this was a unique opportunity. No astronomer had ever seen an impact of two bodies within the solar system.

There was a lot of controversy about what we would see. Everyone had an opinion, including me. I honestly thought that the comet was so small compared to Jupiter that we might see a tiny marking on the face of Jupiter but nothing really obvious. I was willing to be wrong.

Because it was easier to set up and use, AJ Crayon was nice enough to offer his eight-inch Newtonian in his backyard. As the time approached for Comet SL9 to strike Jupiter I started to really anticipate the event. It is always fun when you are going to observe something no living person has viewed before.

The first night we viewed Jupiter trying to observe the effects of the comet strike was Saturday, July 16, 1994. At 9:10 PM MST we were peeking between clouds, and there was a breeze of 10 mph. The equatorial belts on Jupiter were easy to see at 160X. The South Tropical Belt could be seen as faint and thin. The impact site for the "B" fragment was a pretty faint dot two arc seconds in size, very tiny and just south of the South Tropical Zone and north of the South Tropical Belt. This was using 160X and a light-blue filter. We were very happy to realize that there was going to be something to see from the collision.

The next night, Sunday, July 17, 1994, was clouded out by thick clouds and rain.

On Monday, July 18, the good news was there were only a few terrestrial clouds and they seemed to be staying in the distance. The equatorial belts on Jupiter were easy to see at 100X and showed lots of detail at 160X. The South Tropical Belt had several dark markings within it. The equatorial belts had elongated dark markings and a festoon pointing toward the equator. Several impact sites rotated onto Jupiter; they were pretty faint and don't show much contrast. At 9:55 MST we noticed that the limb of Jupiter had a distinct concave area near the South Tropical Belt.

Over the next thirty minutes a tremendous dark marking rotated onto the face of Jupiter. This was the G impact site and was about six arc seconds in size and very dark. The darkest central region was offset toward the equator within the elongated spot. Once it rotated near the equator, we all agreed that it was the most prominent feature we had ever seen on any planet. It was easier to see than Syrtis Major on Mars and darker than the Great Red Spot on Jupiter when it showed its best contrast. It was also noticed that the entire South Tropical region had a dusky hue. This part of Jupiter, where the comet fragments have hit, is medium grey, and its corresponding area in the North Tropical region is a light ivory color.

Jupiter

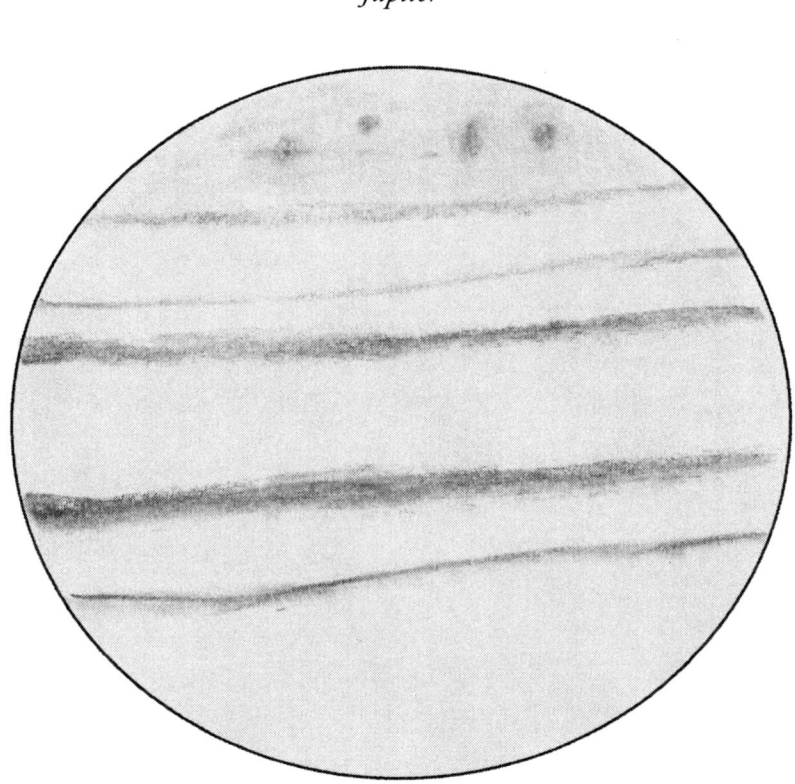

Tuesday, July 19, 1994 at 7:40 MST: The seeing is 5/10 and the transparency is 4/10; there are a few distant clouds and a gentle breeze. Many impact sites come and go across the face of the planet tonight, and at 9:00 PM MST the L site is exiting while the G site is entering and the two dark spots make the appearance of Jupiter a "smiley face" with the two dark spots and two dark Equatorial Belts.

During the evening, Linda Ross, Melissa Weston, and Curt Taylor also observe. Again it is seen that these dark markings are elongated and the darkest central region is offset toward the equator.

Jupiter

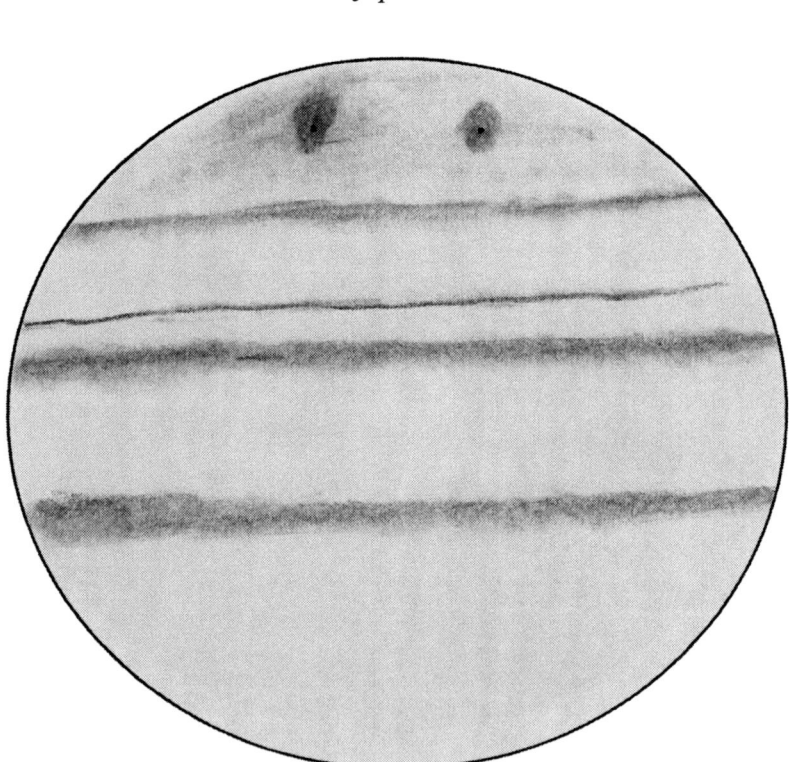

Wednesday, July 20, 1994, at 7:55 MST: The seeing is 2/10 and so is the transparency. The southwestern monsoons are starting up, and

we are observing quickly to get a drawing and observation done before the clouds arrive over the southern horizon. Today is the twenty-fifth anniversary of the Apollo landing on Luna. At 120X, there are four markings across the face of Jupiter. The E, A, C, and P2 markings are lined up in a ragged line from west to east. The E and P2 markings are still quite prominent, but the A and C spots are starting to fade and are pretty difficult to pick out. We can only see these "old" impacts in moments of "not horrible" seeing. When the clouds do finally close in, we tear down the telescope and go watch the Apollo story on television.

Jupiter

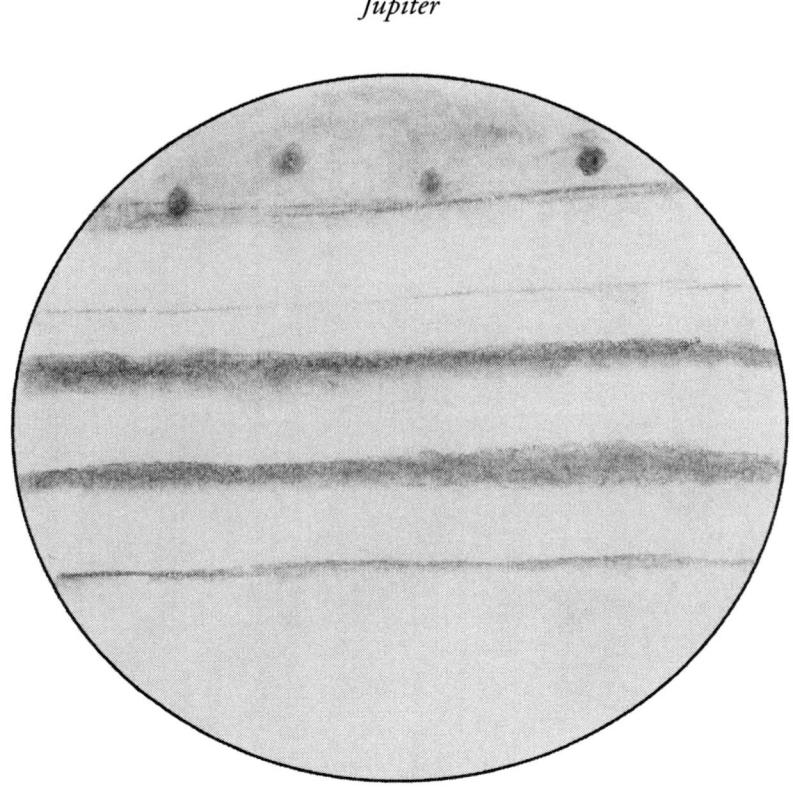

Thursday, July 21, 1994, at 9:00 PM MST: The seeing is 4/10 and the transparency is 2/10 as clouds from a distant thunderhead move across the sky from the south. As the L site rotates off the face of Jupiter, the massive combination impact site of fragments GSRDQ2 is on the central meridian while two other smaller impact areas, N and H, move onto Jupiter. To top off the whole scene the satellite Io is moving behind the planet, and we watch as it slowly disappears behind the blemished face of the King of the Gods. These observations are at 120X and 160X, using a light-blue filter.

Jupiter

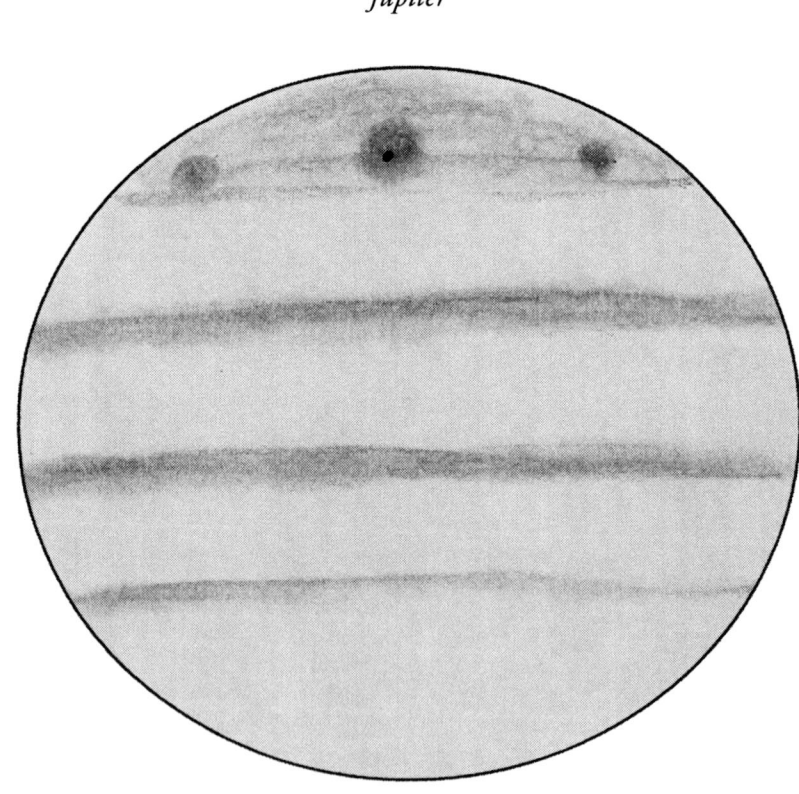

As the thunderstorm covered more of the sky, there came a time when at least 80 percent of the sky was covered in clouds, but the only portion of the sky that was clear is surrounding Jupiter. How lucky can you get? AJ and I found we are getting goose bumps realizing what we were truly observing: a comet that was discovered a year ago was smashing into Jupiter at over one hundred thousand miles per hour and spraying material tens of thousands of miles out from the impact site; the smashed remains of the comet then settled onto the planet and make dark markings that are between one-half and three Earth diameters in size. Absolutely amazing!

Chapter 11: December 29, 1994

Sentinel with Pierre's Twenty-Inch f/5

I had used the thirteen-inch telescope for many years, and like all astronomical mirrors, it eventually needed to be recoated. Exposure to the elements for many nights of observing will eventually tarnish the coating. It was time for the mirror in the thirteen-incher to get a fresh layer of aluminum, so Pierre Schwaar and I took the mirror out of the telescope, boxed it up carefully, and sent it off to a coating service.

A few days after the mirror was on its way, my phone rang and it was Pierre telling me he wanted to go out and do some observing. He offered to bring along his biggest scope, a twenty-inch f/5 on his "Biggest Bigfoot" mount. I jumped at the chance.

We decided to go out to one of our dark sites near the little town of Sentinel, Arizona. It is about one hundred miles from Phoenix and thirty miles from the town of Gila Bend. It turned out that no one else could make it for a two-night observing session, and so it would be just Pierre and me.

Pierre (right) and AJ Crayon. Pierre was born in France, and this is his Napoleon impersonation.

Pierre's twenty-inch scope. He is adjusting the collimation of the primary mirror.

Pierre doing something some people would certainly consider dangerous. He is drawing a sunspot by allowing the image of the sun to fall on the paper and then tracing the sunspot. This is with a twenty-inch telescope. He did not catch anything on fire.

Once the telescope was set up, Pierre made some final collimation adjustments with my help. By this I mean that I moved the adjustment bolts while he observed the glow from the star. Once the star image was perfectly round, the shadow of the secondary mirror was centered and we were ready for a great night of observing. If you own a reflecting scope you will need to get good at collimating. It is not difficult, but it has a learning curve. Find one of several websites that discuss collimation and learn how to do it.

It was one of those observing sessions where everything just worked perfectly. The seeing was eight out of ten, and the transparency was nine out of ten. Clear and steady skies; a rare combination.

Our first target was NGC 7479, a beautiful spiral galaxy in Pegasus. It was pretty bright, large, and elongated 4X1. It had a much brighter core, about 20 seconds across at 165X. This object is a very nice barred spiral, and that structure can be seen on good evenings. The bar is about five arcminutes in length, and each end has a curved glow of an attached spiral arm. It looked like a two-armed garden sprinkler in action. Averted vision made the galaxy grow in size.

NGC 7479

Stephan's Quintet is a grouping of five galaxies in Pegasus. This famous galaxy group is somewhat difficult in telescopes smaller than ten inches aperture. The view gets much better with larger scopes. At 250X in the twenty-inch the fact that this is a group of five galaxies was quite easy to see on this night. There was mottling seen in the two spiral galaxies. Mottling is a texture, somewhat like a quilt, that is seen in the arms of the brightest galaxies. This was my best view of this object ever. No averted vision was needed to acquire or split these galaxies. The smallest galaxy (on the left in the photo) was about four times the size of the seeing disk. The large face-on galaxy had a knot in the arm nearest the tight double galaxy. This feature might be a faint star in the foreground or a bright region within the arm of the galaxy.

Stephan's Quintet

The open cluster M 35 was bright, large, not compressed, and very rich in stars at 100X in the twenty-inch. There was a lovely orange star near the center of the cluster. I counted twenty-eight stars in the northwest quadrant of this cluster, so the total number of stars resolved was over one hundred. I find that it is quick and easy to count one-fourth of a cluster and then multiply by four to get an estimate of the total number of stars seen. When the number of stars seen is overwhelming, this method will at least provide an educated guess.

This cluster was just seen naked eye on that terrific night. In my 10X50 binoculars M 35 was resolved with about twenty stars displayed. Lord Rosse was an Irish nobleman who built the world's largest telescope in 1848; it had a seventy-two-inch mirror. He counted three hundred stars in this cluster. I will check that out when I get my seventy-two-inch working.

M 35

NGC 2158 is the smaller cluster in the field of view with M 35. I saw it as pretty bright, pretty small, very compressed, very rich, and just barely resolved at 100X. Going to 165X brought out more stars. I had seen this cluster with a wedge or arrowhead shape on a variety of nights using many different apertures. The stars filled the field of view, and it was difficult to tell where the cluster ended and the Milky Way began. I counted a total of thirty-two stars involved, including several close double stars.

NGC 2158

NGC 2392 is a famous planetary nebula in Gemini. Its most common name is the "Eskimo Nebula." This is because the detail across the disk of this nebula shows some dark markings that seem like a face and the outer regions are fuzzy, like the fur hood of an Eskimo. At 330X in the twenty-inch the amount of detail across the "face" of this object was fascinating. There were several dark markings that surrounded the central star, and there was an obvious gap between the central disk and the "hood" of material that forms an annulus around the outside. Installing a UHC filter made several of the markings really prominent and enhanced the outer "hood" quite a bit. It was a terrific view of a terrific object, with lots of fine detail.

NGC 2392

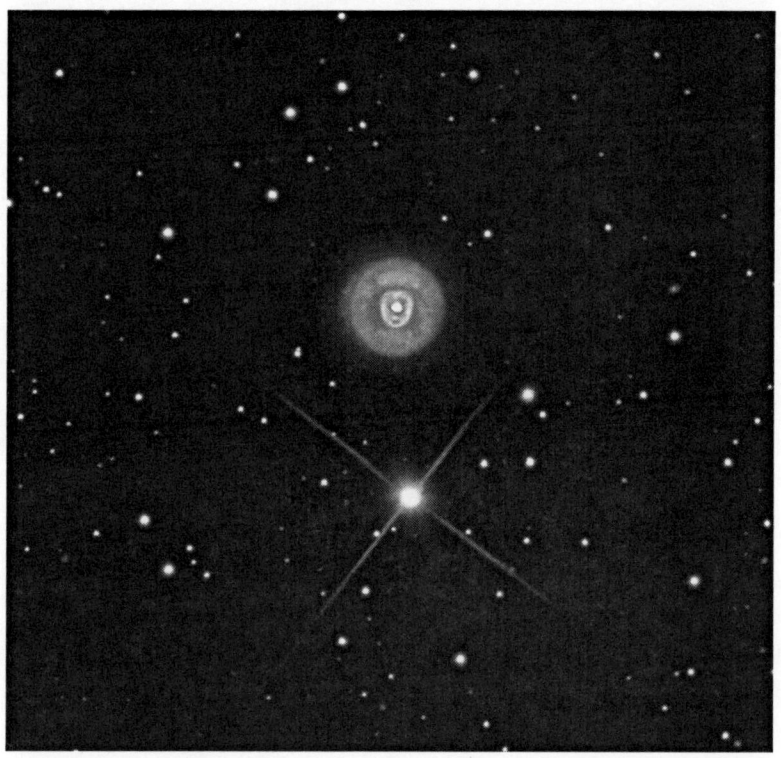

Abell 21 is also a nebula in Gemini, but with a very different shape from the Eskimo. At 165X it was faint, pretty large, and elongated and showed an irregular shape. It was more noticeable at 100X with the UHC filter in place. It had a half-moon shape with the southern end brighter and several stars involved. This is the object marked PK205+14.1 on several star charts. This is a designation from the Perek and Kohoutek list. It is called the Medusa Nebula in Sky Cat 2000, maybe because of the striations that look like Medusa's hair of snakes.

Abell 21

M 1 is the Crab Nebula, one of the most famous supernova remnants in the sky. Supernova explosions happen when stars much larger than the Sun get to a point in their life when they are no longer creating heat in their core. Once this happens, they collapse in on themselves in a few minutes and then explode with violence unknown anywhere on Earth. These massive explosions leave behind a supernova remnant, the gas and dust that used to be included within the star.

Using the twenty-inch at 135X, M 1 was bright, pretty large, elongated, and somewhat brighter in the middle. There were seven stars involved in the nebula, including the neutron star near the middle. The neutron star is the compressed core of the star which exploded. It is a close double star with another stellar point, so high power is needed to see it. Using powers of 330X allowed us to view a brighter inner region and a faint trace of the "Crab" filaments. The filaments were quite low contrast; I saw them more easily with averted vision.

M 1

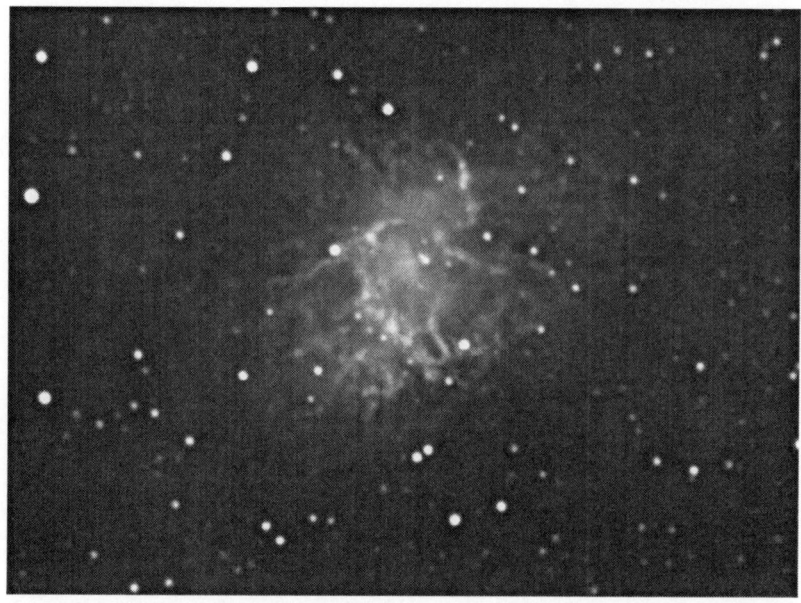

Saving the best for last, we spent nearly an hour on M 42, the famous Orion Nebula. In the widest-field eyepiece we had available, a 38mm giant Erfle, the Orion Nebula was amazing. There was lots of detail in the "wings" of nebulosity above the Trapezium. The inner sections of these wings were a light red or pink color in contrast to the main part of the nebula, which was light green. Moving up to high power with the 6.7mm ultra-wide eyepiece, the central area was fabulous. The southeast side of this area was a straight line with bright nebulosity defining the transition from the inner bright region and the outer fainter nebula. The nebulosity around the Trapezium was still very bright even at high power and was very mottled. Several curved lanes of light and dark nebulosity surrounded the Trapezium, and there were a dozen stars beyond it. This part of the nebula was a light-green color, much like a planetary nebula. The dark "Fish mouth" had scalloped edges and a small amount of glowing nebulosity within this dark area. The three bright stars to the east of the Trapezium had several striking orange stars involved within them. There was another grouping of orange and light orange stars to the south of this area, just at the edge of the field of view. Off to the northwest of the Trapezium was a prominent but thin dark lane that stopped at the area of the bright nebulosity around the Trapezium. This dark lane ran perpendicular to the Fish mouth. All in all, a fascinating and famous region; Pierre and I observed and then rested for a moment and then climbed the ladder to look again at this scene.

M 42

A close-up shot from Jim Barclay in Australia of the area around the Trapezium. The four stars in the middle create the Trapezium figure, and the dark "Fish mouth" is to the left.

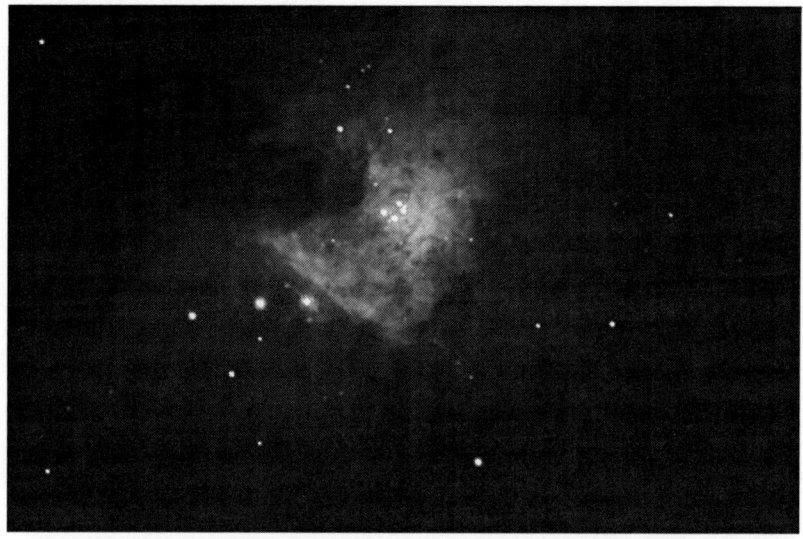

There was no doubt that this was a very memorable viewing session.

Chapter 12: March 27, 1995

Comet Hyakutake

Every once in a while a comet passes by the Earth and shows the beauty of the universe to anyone willing to take the time to view it. Some comets appear in the sky quickly, and others linger around for months. Comet Hyakutake was a quick comet. We first saw it on March 12, and it was going over the horizon by the middle of April. You had to get out there and view or take photos as quickly as you could. So, centered on a great photo session at the end of March, here are my Comet Hyakutake Chronicles:

March 12, 1996: I set up my little six-inch f/6 Newtonian on the sidewalk in front of the house. Using a 14mm eyepiece, a stubby tail is seen and there are two distinct levels of brightness to the coma. The core is very bright and stellar. The entire comet is about thirty arc minutes in size, a nice view from inside the light dome of Phoenix.

I hoped this meant it would be a bright comet later this month. Did my wish ever come true!

March 16, 1996: This observation is from Arizona City, the night of the All Arizona Messier Marathon. I rate the seeing and transparency at 8/10, a superb night. The Saguaro Astronomy Club is the host for over one hundred vehicles filled with astronomers trying to see all the Messier objects in one night. Along with that is this comet, and it is obviously naked eye; I estimate it at third magnitude. There's a beautiful bullet-shaped glow, and I can see two degrees of tail with the naked eye. The large 11X80 finderscope will bring out six degrees of tail, at least two fields of view in the finder. Using the thirteen-inch and a 14mm eyepiece gives 150X and shows off lots of great detail within the coma. I can see three levels of brightness and a blazing, tiny core. A bright ray extends from the coma into the tail.

March 22, 1996: The White Tanks Mountains site is fifty miles from central Phoenix, so it is pretty dark, but not outstanding. The good news is that it is close enough that a one-hour drive gets you to a nice view of the sky and the comet. It is really worth the drive. I rate the seeing at 5/10 and transparency at 6/10. Some clouds were around earlier but now have dissipated.

Using the 22mm Panoptic in the six-inch scope provides a terrific view. The comet tail is obviously a light blue in color; closer to the head of the comet it is turquoise. There is a very bright arc on the leading edge of the comet. The core is a beautiful sunshine yellow in color and a light yellow star, Epsilon Bootis, moves through the tail as the night progresses. The tail is thirty degrees long with the naked eye, a lovely glowing ribbon following a second magnitude core. The 10X50 binoculars offer a splendid view, with ten stars embedded within the comet in and around the coma. I am tired of writing "wow" in my notes.

I am using the tracking mount to shoot some Kodak 400ASA Gold print film. There is a complete set of plans on the SAC website (www. saguaroastro.org). Also on the website are some color photos of this and other objects in this book. To keep the costs down, the book is black and white, except the cover.

The tracking mount

Comet Hyakutake using a 35mm lens and the tracker to keep the stars as small dots rather than lines. Notice the meteor streak in the tail.

March 23, 1996: On this Thursday night, I am alone at the White Tanks site. I decided to load up the "big gun" (the thirteen-inch f/5.6 Newtonian) into the truck and make my way out of town. The night is 7/10 for both seeing and transparency. Even with the wide-field 38mm Erfle eyepiece, this amazing comet fills the field of view. The core is a "comet within a comet"; the tiny nucleus at 60X is also shaped like a comet. There is a fan of material that arcs in the same direction as a bright horseshoe at the front of the coma, and the spike that I have seen several times now is very prominent pointing toward the center of the root of the tail. Going to 330X on the central section of the coma shows lots of detail in this area. The spike is a fountain of comet material that is obviously the beginnings of the tail. This bright region in the core of the comet is a lovely sunshine yellow. This is about the fiftieth comet I have seen in twenty years of observing, and it was really showing off. Not only is the tail thirty degrees long and a light-blue color, but at high power on the core, I can see where the tail is starting out on its journey away from the nucleus.

Comet Hyakutake with a 135mm lens, using the thirteen-inch telescope to track the camera for this five-minute exposure

A drawing with the thirteen-inch scope at 330X

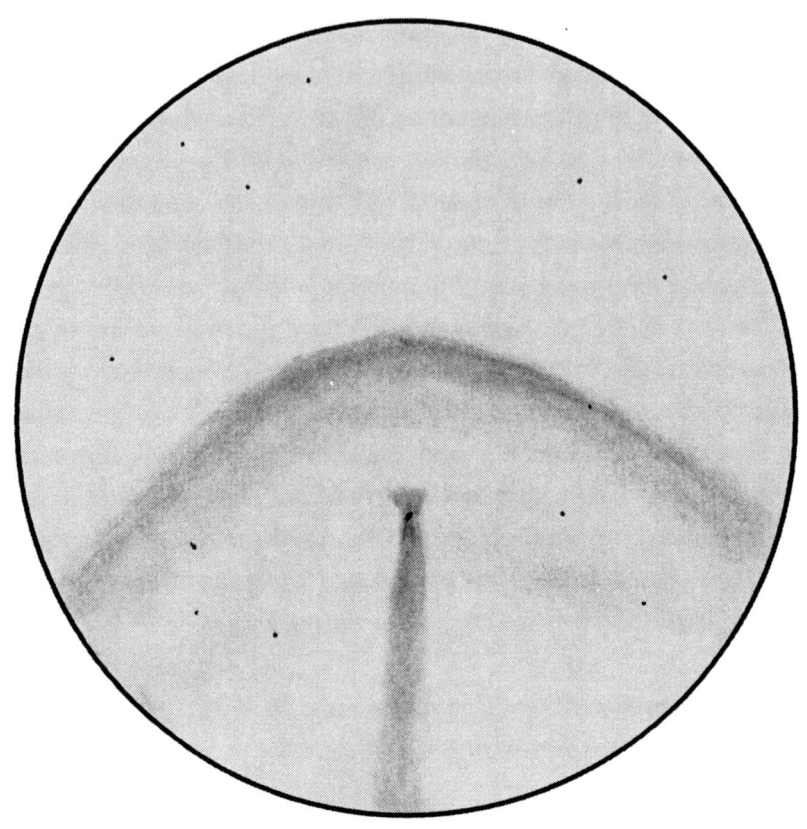

March 24, 1996: I am using the six-inch f/6 at the White Tanks site. Using 25X in the RFT, the comet is still light blue with a turquoise head and golden yellow core—what a sight! At this spot in its journey around the Sun, I see that the coma as surrounded by six stars. With the naked eye I can see thirty-five degrees of tail as this lovely comet makes its way toward the Big Dipper. On Friday night we have a small group at the White Tanks site. AJ and Rich Walker are out enjoying this comet.

March, 27 1996: I am at the White Tanks site with Curt Taylor and Rich Walker, Rich's telescope has a squeak in the declination motor, so when he makes a "dec correction," it makes a short and high-pitched sound. After a few of these, it gets the attention of a small animal in the bushes. When Rich hits the button, the animal responds with a squeak of its own. This "call and response" goes on for a while until I tell Rich that if that thing comes into camp hoping to mate with his scope, I am leaving. A spray of oil is applied and the problem solved.

It was great to share the beauty of this comet with friends and family. I was shooting 400 Fuji print film on the tracker. Curt and I took turns with the 10X50 binoculars and marveled at the beauty of the comet. I was still convinced that the wide-angle view in the binoculars was the best way to look at this comet. The turquoise head and light blue tail were easily seen, and stars of various colors mixed with the tail and coma and then passed through to the other side.

My wife, Linda, and her sister Judy showed up at 2:00 AM for a quick peek. Linda said that it looked like a "beautiful blue rainbow across the sky" and was so in awe that she still thanks me for getting her out of bed in the middle of the night after a long day's work and driving for an hour.

Rich Walker, ready for a night of viewing and photographing the most beautiful comet we have ever seen

April 8, 1996: It's just me. I am waiting to see a much better show than anything on TV. Venus is a searchlight above the western horizon, and Mercury is a smaller spark of light in the orange and yellow bands that are displayed above the desert landscape. Once it starts to get dark, I can see Comet Hyakutake next to the orange star Algol. With the binoculars I can see eight degrees of tail from a comet that still has a turquoise-colored head. What can I say except to repeat that it is so "comet shaped"? As I get better night vision a split in the tail is seen, a division between the dust and ion tails.

The hours passed all too quickly, and I needed to leave this colorful scene to return to the city, but I found that I was cheerful; having spent some time with Mother Nature, dressed in her most lovely outfit.

Chapter 13: October 22, 1995

The Ultimate Star Party

Every once in a while you get an opportunity that you just know will not come around again. For over ten years I wrote articles for the magazine *Amateur Astronomy*. Each article covered objects to view in a constellation that was at its best during that time. The articles were called "What's Up?"—a tribute to astronomy and Bugs Bunny. Tom and Jeannie Clark edited that magazine.

While they were traveling in their motor home they stopped by Arizona for a visit. They told me they were traveling to Texas to attend a get-together called the Ultimate Star Party, a gathering of owners of large telescopes under clear southwestern skies. This star party was organized by Dave Kreige, the owner of Obsession Telescopes.

Yes, I could certainly come along, but how would I get back to Arizona? Once my wife heard that I was willing to take a bus back to Phoenix, she knew that I really wanted to go. And so I slept on the couch in the Clark's motor home for a week and had a wonderful time with a very fun bunch of observers under terrific skies near McDonald Observatory in west Texas.

Tom Clark looking through back issues of Amateur Astronomy *magazine. He was the editor for many years. I had a collection of articles in that magazine.*

Once we arrived at the location of the star party, we started to assemble "the Yard Scope." This huge telescope is a thirty-six-inch f/5 Newtonian. With the help of several others, we pulled the large wooden boxes out of a trailer and started putting them together to form the scope. Once that was done we carefully installed the big mirror into place. Then the tall ladder was set up so that an observer could get to the eyepiece.

Climbing a sixteen-foot tall ladder in the dark to get to the eyepiece of a big telescope is somewhat scary the first few times you do it. You learn to move slowly and only move one limb at a time. It takes a little getting used to, but it is worth it. The views are spectacular. I think it is because when you are on the ladder you are closer to the stars. It certainly feels like it.

I will stick with the one night in the title of this chapter. It was rated at a seven for seeing and a nine for transparency, a "wow" night if there ever was one. The first thing we spotted was Comet Schwassmann-Wachmann 3. It was just seen naked eye and showed a coma and small tail in the 10X50 binoculars. Using the thirty-six-inch telescope it showed a bright spike in the tail.

Me and the thirty-six-inch Yard Scope. The domes of McDonald Observatory are in the background.

It turned out to be a chilly night at six thousand feet altitude in west Texas, so this is me dressed warmly for the evening. Climbing up and down the ladder for the Yard Scope will keep you warmer.

M 57 is the Ring Nebula in Lyra. This famous planetary has been observed many times over the years, and it deserves it. There are few other nebulae that show this kind of detail. Moving up to observing with a telescope as big as the thirty-six-inch showed the central star constantly; it would wink on and off in my thirteen-inch, but it was a light-blue beacon in the big scope. Also, there was a faint outer annulus of nebulosity that could be seen with averted vision. Just glance away from the ring itself and "out of the corner of your eye" this faint outer nebulosity would show up. I found it fascinating to look at the ring directly and then look away as this detail turned on and off.

M 57 Ring Nebula

M 22 is a globular cluster in Sagittarius. Using a 27mm eyepiece showed a glorious cluster with an overwhelming number of stars. There were several dark markings within five arc minutes of the center of the cluster and three small groupings of ten pretty faint stars that are clusters within a cluster. I do believe that globulars are the type of object that really "show off" in a large telescope. These amazingly large balls of stars are phenomenal with a large scope. I counted 105 stars in the NW quadrant of the cluster. Therefore, the entire cluster was showing over 400 members.

M 22 cluster in Sagittarius

NGC 6888 is a "Wolf-Rayet Bubble" in Cygnus. WR (Wolf-Rayet) stars are very large and hot. These stars are constantly spewing off their outer layers of gas and dust. Then the hot core of the star lights up the gas cloud by a process called photoionization. The energetic radiation from the star knocks electrons away from the gaseous atoms. As the electrons recombine with these atoms they give off light, much like a neon bulb. In NGC 6888 this gas forms a beautiful arching shape that gives it the name "the Crescent Nebula." The bright star at the center of the crescent is the WR star.

With a 20mm eyepiece and a UHC filter this object took up the entire field of view. The large crescent shape showed a knot of eight stars on the top side. There were areas of smooth nebula and areas that showed texture. Beyond NGC 6888 on all sides there were several faint nebulae for which I cannot find a designation.

NGC 6888, the "Wolf-Rayet Bubble," in Cygnus

NGC 6992 is the brightest portion of the Veil Nebula in Cygnus. Using a 27mm eyepiece and a nebular filter showed an amazing amount of detail within this object. It was five eyepiece fields in length, so the observer must move the telescope along its length to see the entire supernova remnant. Just thinking about the fact that I was viewing the material created in the explosion of a star is fascinating.

It looked like the result of a three-dimensional taffy machine. Some portions showed mottling, and some were smooth sections with stars involved of a wide variety of magnitudes. There were several places where you could see small chunks of nebulae detached from the main body of the Veil. We gave up trying to come up with superlatives about this object in the thirty-six-inch. We each climbed up and down the ladder three or four times to become enraptured by this fascinating object. This was my finest view of any object at any time in any telescope.

NGC 6992 taken by Paul Lind with a twelve-inch f/3.6 astrograph that he constructed

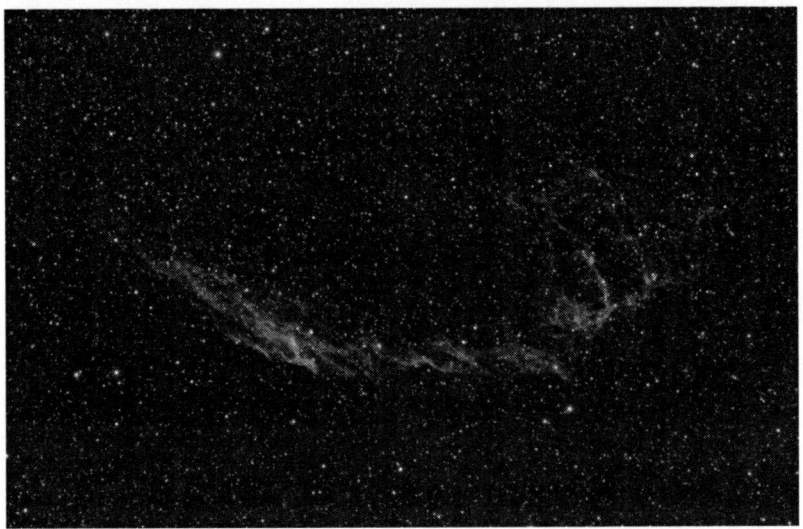

NGC 1535 is a round, quite symmetrical planetary nebula in Eridanus. Using a 12mm eyepiece showed a bulls-eye of nebulosity, with the inner ring as light green and a light-red outer fringe. The central star was easy and had a very thin dark region surrounding the central star. There was a very faint star involved at the edge of the nebula.

NGC 1535, a planetary nebula in Eridanus

NGC 1365 is a spiral galaxy in Fornax, far to the south. Viewing in Dave Kreige's twenty-five-inch telescope with a 7mm eyepiece, it was very bright and pretty large, and the spiral structure was obvious. The dark lane in the central core could be seen about 50 percent of the time. I saw the core is elongated 1.8X1, and a dark lane cut through it. There were several bright knots and some mottling in the arms, which extended out from a central bar. There were two faint galaxies in the field of view.

My drawing of NGC 1365, showing the easily seen "water sprinkler" form of this barred spiral galaxy

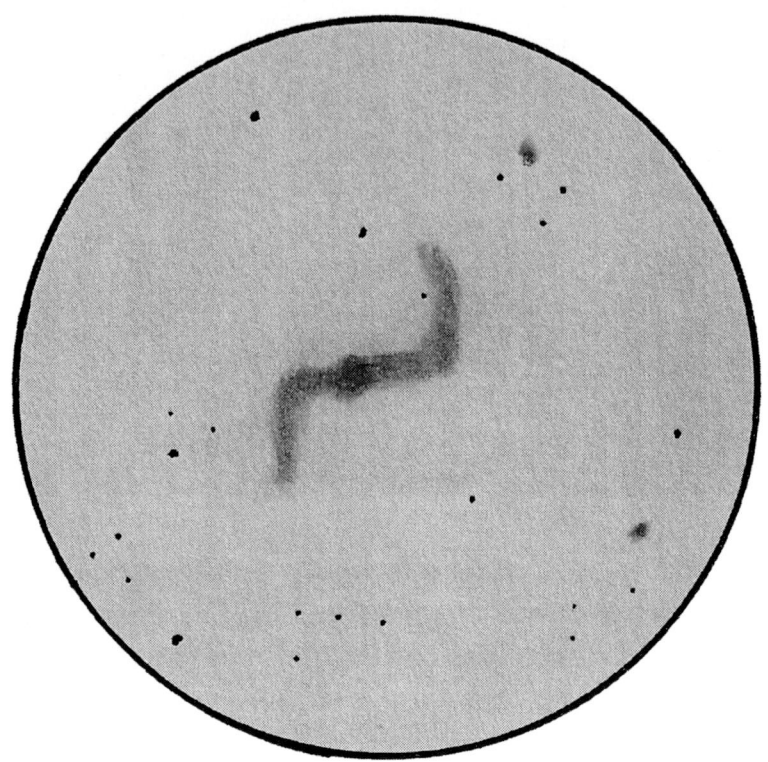

Galaxy clusters are fascinating in large telescopes; this is where large instruments make a rather ordinary part of the sky into something fascinating. Galaxy clusters form in the same way as star clusters. Remember that gravity only pulls things together, so the stars or galaxies are inexorably pulled close to one another. The only place where anti-gravity exists is on *Star Trek*.

Many of the most prominent galaxy clusters were discovered by George Abell in his searches done on the wide-field Schmidt camera plates taken in the 1950s at Mt. Palomar.

Abell 426 is a galaxy cluster in Perseus. Using the thirty-six-inch and a 20mm eyepiece I counted seventeen bright galaxies and fifty-eight other, fainter members. All these galaxies were within one field of view of the central section. Most of the galaxies were round or slightly elliptical; a few showed faint spiral structure. This was a pretty rich star field, and so there were lots of stars and galaxies all bunched together. There were two NGC galaxies, NGC 1270 and NGC 1275, that were the middle of this galaxy cluster. Just north of them was Tom Clark's "River of Galaxies," a long chain of galaxies that stretched out of the field of view. Once you see it, you can't forget it.

Abell 426, a galaxy cluster in Perseus

M 33 is the Pinwheel Galaxy in Triangulum. In the thirty-six-inch f/5 with a 27mm eyepiece it is amazing. The detail that could be seen within the arms of this face-on galaxy equaled what can be seen in photographs from the forty-eight-inch Schmidt camera;

it was undrawable. The curved arms were filled with bright spots from the core to the tips of the spiral. I counted twenty bright areas in the arm, which I saw as "up." I could see the difference between Population I and Population II areas in the galaxy. The stars in the core formed a smooth surface to the central section that is light yellow, whereas the arms were splotchy and bluish. Being able to see the two different types of stellar populations with my eye was truly a unique experience.

M 33, the Pinwheel Galaxy in Triangulum

And all too soon it was over. I sat on the bus returning to the "real world." Fortunately, there was no one in the seat next to me and I had the time to organize my notes and relive viewing, drawing, and enjoying all these fabulous deep-sky goodies. It was a week that will live in my memory forever.

CHAPTER 14: APRIL 12, 1997

ᴄᴍ

COMET HALE-BOPP
PUBLIC VIEWING

It all started six months before the date given for this chapter. During New Moon observing sessions under dark skies Comet Hale-Bopp was brightening up and beginning to form its coma. As the ice and dust was being puffed away from the nucleus of the comet it was growing in size and brightness every time we observed it. There was chatter that this had the potential to be a great comet.

After viewing and photographing Comet Hyakutake the previous year, we were ready. We had gotten some good shots of that beautiful comet and knew that if Hale-Bopp got to naked-eye brightness we would be prepared to get some good photos.

Before we get to the story of the public viewing session let me tell you what we saw before that evening.

On Feb. 14, 1997, I slept for a short while and then made my way into the desert forty miles north of Phoenix to photograph and observe Comet Hale-Bopp. It was quite breezy, five to ten mph steady and gusting to twenty mph. Observing the comet was fun, however, and in the 10X50 binoculars it had a tail that I estimated at six degrees. The north side, which had the ion tail involved, was much brighter than the rest of the comet. There was a dark division down the middle of the tail, probably the shadow of the nucleus.

The Comet Hale-Bopp using a 55mm lens, a two-minute exposure on Fuji 800 film

This comet really shows off the fact that there are two types of tails on comets. A dust tail is just that, particles of dust about the consistency of cigar smoke. This tail is white or ivory-colored in a photo and will curve as the solar wind pushes it away from the sun. An ion tail is made up of atoms and molecules that have been ionized by the energetic particles from the Sun. These particles strike the atoms of oxygen, nitrogen, and other elements. When the atoms are struck they give off an electron and take on a positive charge. They become ions; hence the name. This tail is usually blue in color and is straight back from the nucleus.

Moving up to the thirteen-inch f/5.6 at 100X the core showed an amazing wealth of detail. A lot of bright material was boiling off the core in a wide fan of dust and gas that wrapped up and over to form a hood of bright material that appears "in front" of the nucleus. At 220X the nucleus was elongated 2X1 and the fan of material was quite prominent. There was also a thin spike of material on the other side of the core.

I still love it with the naked eye; it is just plain fun to look up from observing a cluster or nebula with the telescope and see a bright comet making its way through the familiar Cygnus Milky Way. It is still funny that the constellation of Sagitta, the Arrow, points almost right at the comet. Is this a celestial "look here" marker?

A trip to see the comet on February 19, 1997, a Wednesday morning, showed off the fact that Comet Hale-Bopp was increasing in brightness and growing a longer tail as time went on. In my 10X50 binoculars the ion tail on the north side of the comet was eight degrees long, the first four degrees of which was pretty easy to see and the last four increasingly more difficult as it blends in with the Milky Way. I estimated the brightness of this comet at magnitude 2.0 using Gamma Cygni and Deneb as the reference stars.

Moving up to the thirteen-inch scope at 100X showed a wealth of detail around the nucleus. The persistent fan-shaped fountain on the south side of the nucleus was even more prominent! It sprayed off material and made the south side of the dust tail *much* brighter than the north side. Going to 150X with a 14mm Meade UWA eyepiece showed that the fan of material had several bright and dark areas that appeared much like the mottled arm of a spiral galaxy.

Was there really a month left for this comet to get bigger and brighter? This was going to be great!

A shot of Hale-Bopp taken with a 35mm lens and then fired a flash gun to light up the saguaro cactus during a two-minute exposure. The color version of this photo is the cover of this book. It is called "Goalposts."

My dad, David Coe Jr., travels to Arizona each spring to visit with me and watch some spring training baseball games with his beloved Seattle Mariners. Maybe next year, Dad.

Regardless of baseball hopefuls, I talked my dad into coming out with me for a view of the comet. On March 6, 1997, a Thursday morning, we went to a spot about thirty miles from Phoenix set up and ready to go.

That morning Comet Hale-Bopp was great. I estimated the magnitude at 0.8 and tail at five degrees long with the naked eye and ten degrees long in the 10X50 binoculars. The blue ion tail was within the wide dust tail and showed really high surface brightness. Using my six-inch f/6 at 40X it was a great sight, with lots of material boiling off the core and the intertwined tails coming off the nucleus. Going to 100X showed the concentric arcs of comet stuff near the core that had persisted for several days.

My dad, AJ, and I were all fascinated with the comet. It was bright and easy to see with the naked eye and showed lots of detail in a simple pair of binoculars. It was a memorable night for me to be able to show my father such an excellent comet.

My observing buddy, AJ Crayon, his eight-inch Newtonian telescope with a camera on the back, and Comet Hale-Bopp in the distance. A cloud cuts through the comet.

With all that as a build-up, let's get on to the public star party. The Saguaro Astronomy Club (SAC) has held public viewing sessions for over twenty years. We dearly love to show off the sky to people who have rarely, or never, looked through a telescope before. It is a joy to share the sky with enthusiastic newcomers.

And now we had a big, bright comet to attract lots of people to observe. We had no idea what we were getting into. We advertised like crazy and were on the TV news, newspapers, and radio and sent flyers to people in all types of education from kindergarten to college.

We showed up early and found that we had over thirty telescopes all set up and ready to go as the Sun disappeared over the horizon. And then the crowds started to arrive. By 8:00 PM we had lines of thirty to fifty people at every telescope. Two friends of mine told me that all the parking for a mile around was jam-packed. The park ranger who was helping us called the police and told them that he needed help

with the traffic control. I guess that some officers showed up and got the cars parked in such a way that they did not stop traffic. We showed a lot of people the sky that night, and many thanked us repeatedly for setting up the telescopes and allowing so many to view the comet.

A girl looking through the thirteen-inch telescope at Comet Hale-Bopp. It is a twenty-second photograph.

I have no doubt that I showed the comet to over four hundred people that night. There was a line at all times until nearly 11:00 PM when we finally started to dismantle the scopes and go home. What a night!

This is not a daylight photo. The Moon is about half full and is located behind the camera. This is a thirty-second image of the crowd at the SAC public viewing session with Comet Hale-Bopp overhead.

We have continued to have a public viewing session since Hale-Bopp appeared to the present. There are always at least two hundred people ready to show up and observe. We do get a few new club members from the group, but that is not the point. We are offering the universe, and there is no substitute for viewing the universe with your own eyes.

Chapter 15: February 26, 1998

Eclipse Cruise: SS *Dawn Princess*

Before February of 1998 the Saguaro Astronomy Club was filled up with people who had never seen a total solar eclipse. After that date, that statement was no longer the truth. I have always been proud of my astronomy club, but this adventure really was the icing on the cake. In a club of about one hundred members we had twenty-two folks pay to travel by airliner and then cruise ship to get into the path of a total solar eclipse.

The most expensive observing accessory I have ever used: the SS Dawn Princess

2 25 '98

There are two types of eclipses: lunar and solar. A lunar eclipse happens when the light from the Sun is blocked off from reaching the Moon by having the Earth pass directly between the Sun and Moon. So the full Moon turns very dark for an hour or two. As the Moon dims it also turns red because the light from the Sun passes through the atmosphere of the Earth and gets reddened before illuminating the Moon. The good news if you are trying to view a lunar eclipse is that they can be viewed by the entire hemisphere of the Earth that is facing the Moon, so lots of people have viewed a lunar eclipse. Just go outside when one happens and you and half the people on Earth will have a view of the full Moon fading out and changing color.

A total solar eclipse is a very different event. From the point of view of someone on Earth, the Moon blocks off the Sun and daylight is radically dimmed until it appears like twilight outside—a very impressive sight! To view a total solar eclipse you must be at the right location at the right time. The path of the eclipse averages fifty miles wide at best, and the eclipse cannot last longer than about seven minutes. So a solar eclipse demands some real planning.

A few of the club members decided to stay put on the Caribbean island of Aruba, and the rest sailed along on the SS *Dawn Princess*. It is very nice to view an eclipse only 150 feet from the buffet.

I will get to the eclipse in a moment, but the other thing that worked out well was viewing the sky from the deck of a ship cruising the Caribbean. Because we were far to the south of Arizona, parts of the sky were available for viewing that never gets above the horizon in the US southwestern deserts.

I found that if I kept my feet firmly planted wide apart I could move with the ship and use my 10X50 binoculars to see quite a bit of detail. We quickly found a location on the ship that was perfect. It was at the forward end of the ship, near the bow. Because it was ten decks above the main deck, we called it "Ten Forward." Because the *Starship Enterprise* in *Star Trek, the Next Generation* had its bar on a deck location named Ten Forward, we were hooked. Sorry; if you are not a trekkie the joke will elude you. Don't worry; be happy.

From this Ten Forward location we viewed the night sky as we sailed around from island to island. Then we planned to view the eclipse from there once eclipse day arrived. For a week the ship pulled into several exotic ports: Aruba and the Virgin Islands.

Because the ship was moving, I could not take photos of these deep-sky objects; their images will be presented in the chapter on my trips to Australia.

Viewing with the naked eye, this darkened part of the ship allowed me to get somewhat dark adapted. The Milky Way was a wide glowing arch from the tail of Canis Major through the False Cross in Vela and over to the glow of Eta Carina, then on to Crux. Because there was a light haze near the water, the Milky Way was not as bright as when seen at Sentinel, Arizona, but it was easy to see and showed a few dark lanes. The star clusters around Eta Carina were easy. The top star in Crux was obviously orange, even to the naked eye. Comparing to Betelgeuse, it was about the same orange color, even if a fainter star.

The Eta Carina nebula was the most obvious naked-eye bright spot in the Milky Way. It was cut almost in half by a dark lane. The outer nebula really showed up with averted vision. In the 10X50 binoculars I could see twelve stars involved with a hint of more.

IC 2602 is the southern most of the three clusters that surround Eta Carina. In the binoculars I could see eleven stars in two groups; this cluster was split down the middle by a dark lane. NGC 3114 was compact and pretty small but pretty bright. Saving the best for last, NGC 3532 was an excellent cluster, one of the best in all the sky. This bright and compact group of stars will show about ten stars that are held steady and another ten suspected. There was a hint of a dark lane penetrating the cluster in a dense region. This was a showpiece. This area was obviously the brightest part of the Milky Way that was above the horizon. I really needed some sleep, so off to the cabin I went.

A photo I took from Australia of the Eta Carina Nebula and two of the clusters surrounding it. IC 2602 is below the nebula, and NGC 3532 is to the left. This photo is a twelve-minute exposure with a 135mm lens.

At 2:15 AM I was all alone. The objects from the previous observing session were setting. The Southern Cross, the constellation of Crux, was now unmistakable. The Jewel Box cluster showed six stars in the binoculars, but there were no colors seen in these stars. Obviously the star colors needed the aperture of a telescope, an impossible task on the moving deck of a ship. The dark Coal Sack nebula could be seen with the naked eye but was better in binoculars. Again, there was poor contrast near the ocean haze.

With the naked eye I noticed two things I had never seen before: First, the ship was on course directly at Scorpius. The bright orange star Antares was right over the masthead on the bow. Second, I had never seen the stars of the constellation of Centaurus so bright—they were spectacular. I could see thirty-five to forty stars of magnitudes two to five that were very obvious in this area of the sky. I could only think of the constellation of Orion as a part of the sky with as many bright stars concentrated in one area.

On the date of the eclipse the captain carefully positioned the ship for clear sky and maximum eclipse duration. This involved steering the ship through a "squall line," a band of dark rain clouds. As the drizzle started up, the spirits of a shipload of astronomers sank. But as we cleared the clouds, the rain ceased and clear blue sky was on the other side. There was an audible sigh of relief. The good news was that there were no other problems with clouds for the rest of the eclipse.

The shadow of the Moon made its way across the Caribbean Sea and engulfed us in darkness. To the unaided eye there was a hole in the sky where a crescent Sun had been a few seconds earlier. Once the Moon completely covered the disk of the Sun, the beautiful pearlescent corona was obvious. The corona is the outer atmosphere of the Sun and stood out about one solar radius on all sides, with a few streamers extending the corona even further out, as much as two solar radii. A bright prominence was easily seen on the top side of the dark disk.

The sky brightness was about the same as deep twilight, so several planets were seen during this particular eclipse. Mercury was "above and to the left" of the Sun, and Jupiter was straight below. Jupiter was a little brighter than Mercury, approximately one magnitude. Brilliant Venus stood well above the western horizon. I had to remind myself not to think of it as an airplane landing light, but it never moved during totality. The striking feature of this eclipse was the brilliant planets setting off the totally eclipsed Sun.

After soaking up the view with the naked eye view for thirty seconds or so, a little voice in my head said, "You have binoculars," and I suddenly remembered to use my 10X50 optical aid. The scene was perfectly framed in the binoculars, Mercury at eleven o'clock and Jupiter at six. Maybe we should call this the "five minutes to six" eclipse? The binoculars also show a wealth of detail within the corona. The streamers had delicate detail that reminded me of the glint of sunlight through a spider web. The bright prominence was small but prominent.

After using the binoculars for thirty seconds or so, that little voice said, "You really ought to finish off that roll of film." So I returned to the camera. My observing partner for over twenty years was next to me, and Dave Fredericksen said he was getting good shots with the 800mm setup he was using. Knowing that Dave was getting good close-ups, I decided to zoom out to 150mm for the wider-angle view, and I shot a variety of exposures. I thought of saving a shot for the diamond ring, but as I tried to wind the film I had exhausted the roll.

David and his photo setup

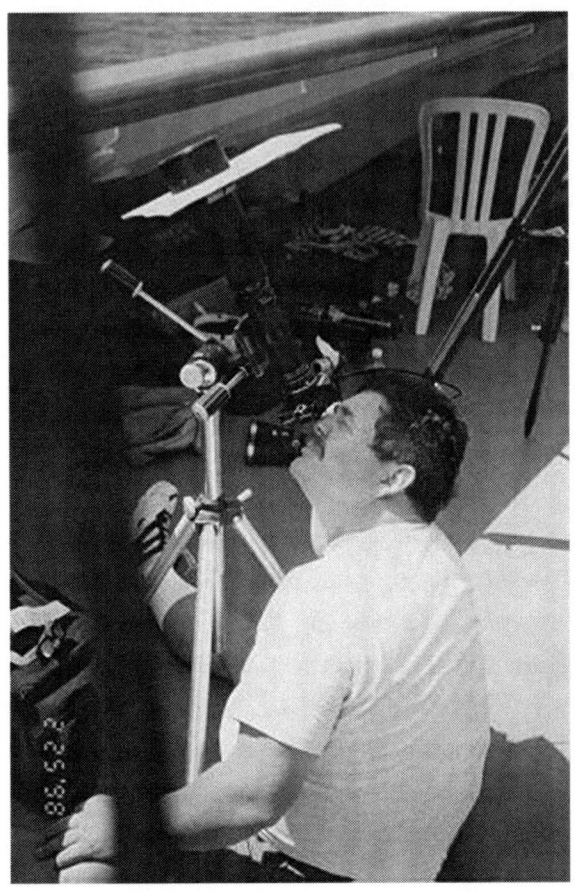

I returned to view with the binoculars, and ten seconds after getting the 10X50s up to my eyes third contact began. This means that the Sun was starting to show itself though the valleys on the Moon. Baily's Beads were seen for five seconds or so as a string of tiny pearls along the bottom of the Moon. Then the diamond ring effect lit up the edge of the Sun-Moon conjunction. This brilliant flame of light grew and grew. Again, the little voice said, "You're going to hurt yourself," and I deliberately removed the binoculars from my eyes.

*The diamond ring effect lighting up the edge
of the Sun-Moon conjunction*

I used a small tape recorder to record the reactions of the people around me and of course, myself. I was surrounded by family and friends, thinking that after a short time during the eclipse we would settle down and give a rational account of what was happening around us and the sights we observed. That rationale returned after a while, but during the eclipse the only rational utterances are, "Wow, will you look at *that!*"

The SAC members at Ten Forward

I had been an active observer of the skies for over twenty years, and there was no spectacle in Nature that I had ever seen that was anything like a total solar eclipse. The eerie lighting effects, planets easily seen at two o'clock in the afternoon, and the lovely translucent corona fanning out from the black disk of the eclipsed Sun were unique and magnificent.

My Mom, trying to "win back the price of the cruise." Yea, right. She did manage to pull herself away from the casino long enough to enjoy the eclipse.

As always, the public is quite uninitiated when it comes to what to expect. On Friday, after the eclipse, David and I were in the elevator of the *Dawn Princess* with a woman who looked at David's eclipse T-shirt and inquired if we were astronomers. We answered yes, and she said, "It was lovely. Does every cruise get an eclipse?"

It was a cruise, after all: my wife, Linda, with lots of hungry fish. If you snorkel with fish food in your hands, they will find you.

CHAPTER 16: OCTOBER 17, 1999

ᴄᴍ

A NIGHT IN THE OBSERVATORY

My message for this chapter is that if you have a chance to build an observatory, then do it. Mine was a simple roll-off roof style. The roof is on rollers and moves out of the way to allow the telescope to view the sky. It took my contractor a little while to get used to that idea. I would talk about the roll-off roof and then discuss the size of the building. Then he would stop me and say, "So the roof is going to roll off?" After a few minutes searching among some books I found some plans and photos of the type of observatory I wanted, and then he understood. It is difficult to picture in your head what you have never seen.

The construction went well, and in a couple of weeks it was all set up and I was ready to install the seven-inch Maksutov telescope I planned to use in the observatory. I knew it did a great job on the Moon and planets. From within the light dome of Phoenix I knew that would be the major use of this scope.

A construction photo of the observatory

The complete observatory

The seven-inch Maksutov telescope I installed in the observatory

I found that it was great to have an observatory at my back door. If you are hungry, fix a sandwich; tired, take a nap; cold, go inside and warm up. I installed a computer and a speaker system so I could listen to some music while viewing. The walls blocked off direct light from my neighbors and blocked out the wind as well.

I had everything at my fingertips. It was very nice to have a Moon map or list of double stars to observe right in the observatory. I just flipped a couple of switches, rolled back the roof, put in an eyepiece, and I was observing. You can't beat it.

The more I observed the more I realized how much I could do, even from a light-polluted backyard. I followed the satellites of Jupiter, watched the rings of Saturn open and close, split many hundreds of double stars, and viewed the brightest red carbon stars all around the sky.

I bought a simple camera that allowed me to take images of a variety of these objects. All the major suppliers of astronomy equipment will sell you a solar system camera—mine was a Phillips ToUCam. With an adaptor it slid right into the scope like an eyepiece. Some simple programs allowed me to take several seconds of images and then stack them together to make sharper images. I will not spend lots of time on the techniques; there are several books on the subject.

One of my favorite areas of the Moon, the Bay of Rainbows or Sinus Iridium

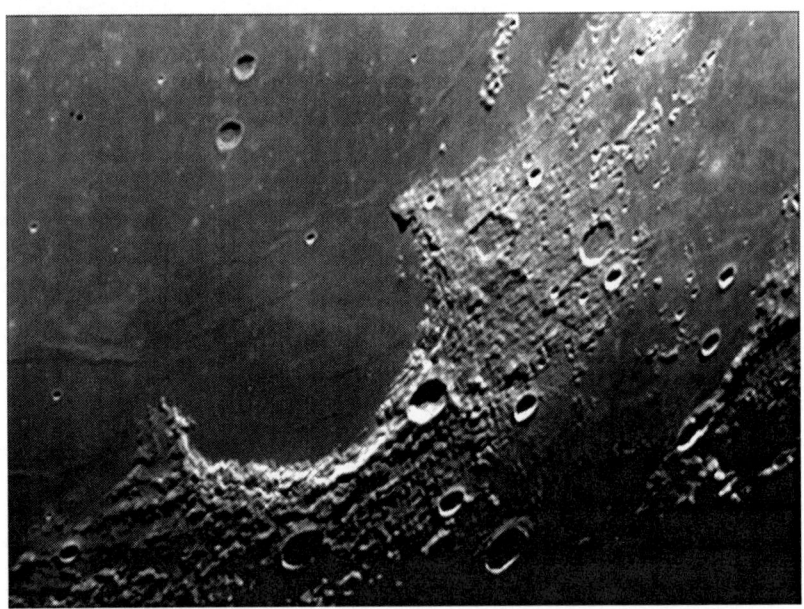

The lunar feature I call the Straight Wall; the scientific name is Rupes Recta.

A drawing of Jupiter at 260X with a blue filter installed. There is a dark shadow of the satellite Io on the disk.

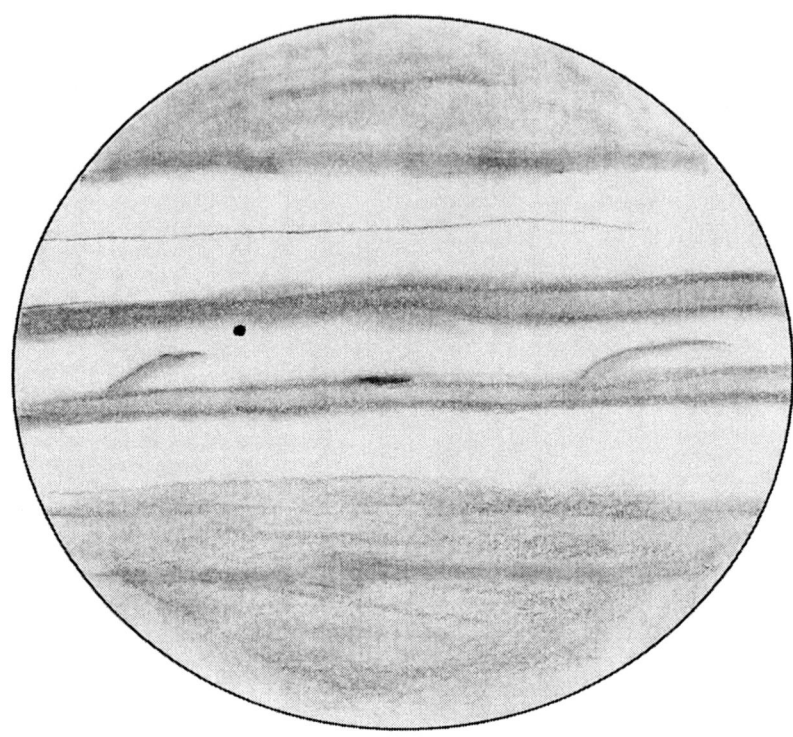

My best image ever of Saturn. It consists of over one hundred images stacked together. The dark lane in the rings is called the Cassini Division.

I have many hours of great memories of being out in the observatory alone around midnight. The seeing has settled down, so I can use higher magnifications and see lots of detail on the Moon or whatever planet is in good viewing position. There are always more multiple stars to view. Our neighbor has a tree that houses an owl and her family. Often she will hoot at me and the rest of the world as I watch the universe twirl overhead.

CHAPTER 17: NOVEMBER 18, 2001

LEONID METEOR STORM

Meteor showers are easy to observe; no optical equipment is needed. A telescope or even binoculars provide too narrow a field of view to observe these streaks of light. All you need is a comfortable chair, something to keep you warm, and a location that will allow you to observe a large part of the sky. This meteor shower is called the Leonids because they appear to come from the constellation of Leo, the Lion.

Because the Leonid meteor shower is a somewhat rare event, I had planned to make a long drive far from the city lights. But sometimes things just don't work the way you plan. It turned out that David Fredericksen and I had to work on the Monday that followed the Leonids, and so we were going to have to stay in close to town. We drove out at midnight because meteor showers are always better after local midnight.

Let me explain that. The meteors are small bits of a comet that are still in orbit around the Sun. When these tiny grains of a comet tail encounter the Earth's atmosphere they disintegrate and leave a bright trail of light that is called a meteor. You may have heard it spoken of as a shooting star.

Because they are in predictable orbits there are specific evenings to go out and view a meteor shower. The Leonids are always on November 18, or close to that date depending on the movement of the stream of meteors. When the Earth is turning into the meteor stream there will be more meteors in the sky, and that is always after midnight. That is when the rotation of the Earth is taking an observer into the path of the most meteors.

One more part to the explanation is that there will be no meteorites from these meteor showers. The material in orbit has about the consistency of your fingernails and so will not survive the encounter with the Earth's atmosphere. What are streaking overhead are small meteoroids that are completely destroyed by their passage through the air.

So now it was 2:00 AM and David and I were at a spot about forty miles north of Phoenix. There were distant clouds, but Leo was up so the radiant (the place in the sky that is the starting point of the meteor shower) was well above the horizon. And the shower was starting. We saw lots of meteors, hundreds per hour at least. About 10 percent were bright fireballs that light up the sky. The best time wouldn't occur for another hour, and it was already the best meteor shower I had ever seen.

At 3:00 AM, and we decided to do a real count of the meteors. We sat back to back and David set his watch to chime in one minute. In one minute we saw twenty meteors; with sixty minutes in an hour that equals 1,200 meteors per hour. Now we were really getting excited, and the bright streaks across the sky just kept on coming.

The photos I tried to take were mediocre at best. Here are two sketches I made that night. I tried to provide some idea of how the meteor shower appeared. As I looked down at the paper to put a bright meteor onto the sketch, I would miss a dozen or more while in the best part of the shower. I tried to give the impression of an exploding meteor with the "starburst" at the end of the fireballs. One drawing is centered on Leo, the other on Orion.

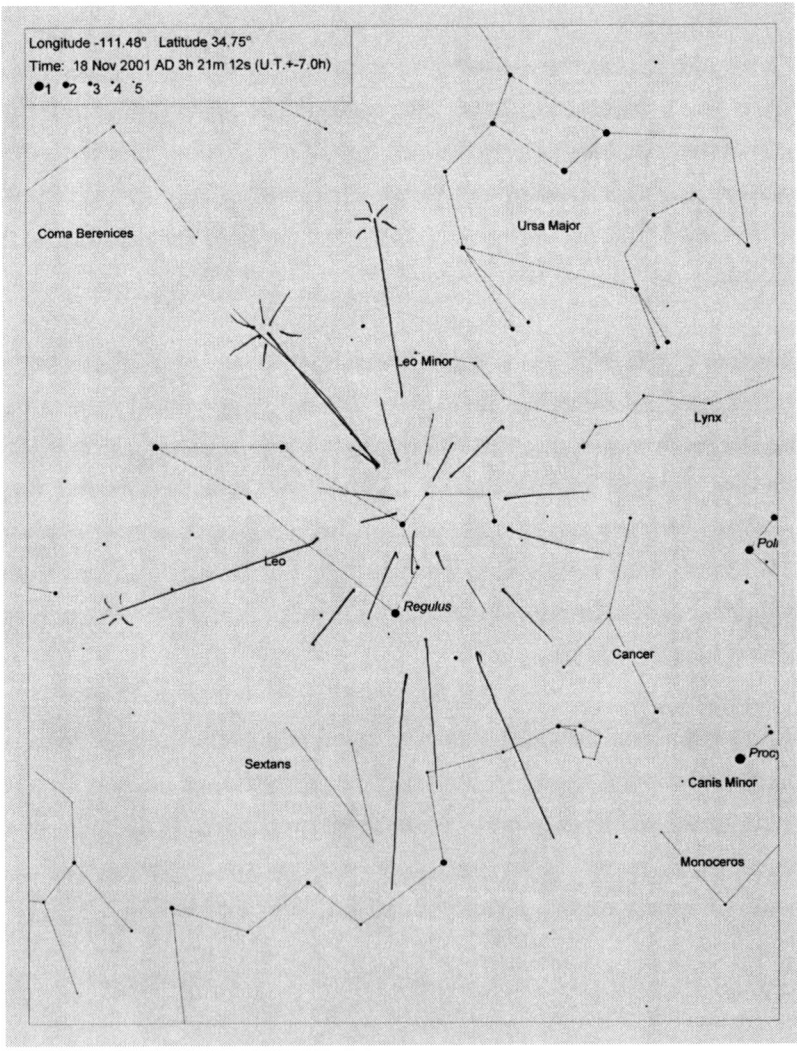

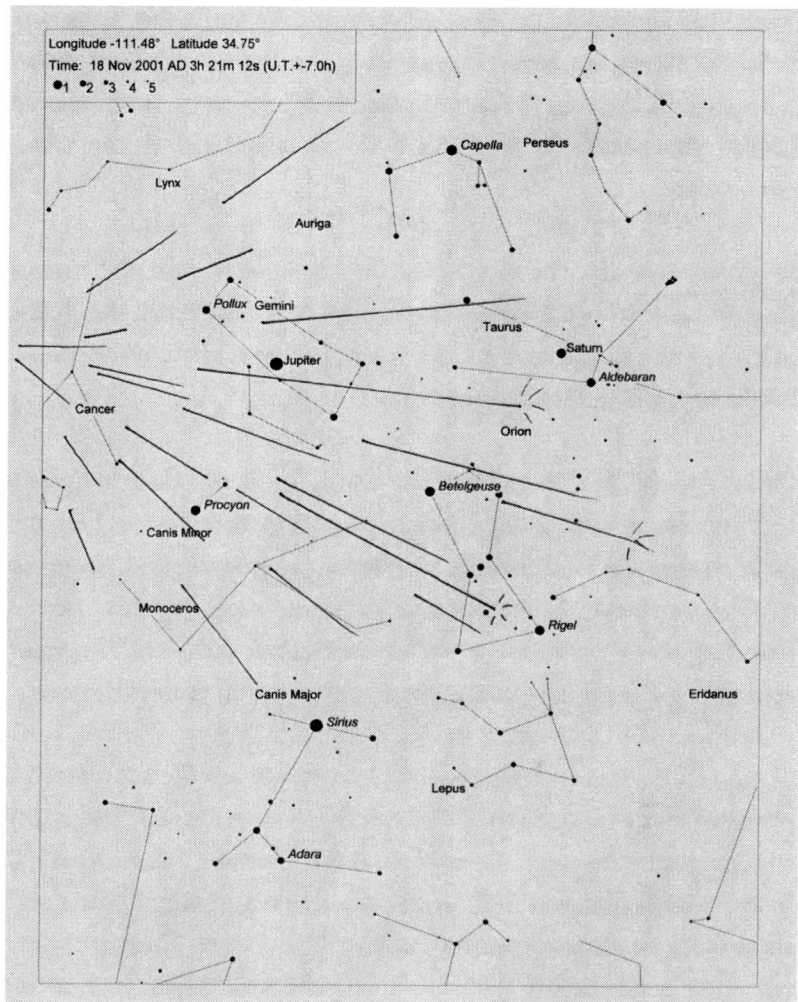

Listening to each of us shout out, "Oh boy," or just plain, "Wow," over and over is an indication of just how overwhelming this meteor storm was at providing a sky show. It was like nothing we had ever seen before. At one point I saw four really bright meteors in less than a minute, which just does not happen on a regular night of viewing the sky.

I used the binoculars to view a bright smoke trail from a meteor. It stayed lit up for five minutes after the fireball streaked across from Leo all the way to Gemini. In the binoculars I could see the smoke trail twist and move as it slowly dissipated in the upper atmosphere.

At about 4:40 AM the clouds started to move in and the meteor shower was getting a little less impressive. As we folded up the chairs, put away the blankets, and got ready to leave, there were several bright fireballs as if to say good-bye.

Okay, I wrote all that and it is the truth, but it still does not give a real impression of what it is like to witness a meteor shower. I am not positive that words, drawings, or photos can provide that. So much of what we observe in the sky either does not move or moves slowly. Planets rise and set at the rate of fifteen degrees per hour. To see the movement of a planet among the distant stars takes days or weeks.

The quick flash of a meteor is just plain fun to watch, and there are plenty of meteor watchers out there. It is just amazing and fascinating to view over a thousand meteors per hour; there are "shooting stars" in every direction you look in the sky. Even a modest shower will show off these glowing portions of the solar system. There are about ten other good meteor showers during the year. Make time to see one.

The meteor storm aspect of the Leonids returns in November of the year 2033. I hope that there is a time in your life where you are fortunate enough to be under the kind of meteor storm we saw on that amazing night.

CHAPTER 18: APRIL 14, 2002

◆

MESSIER MARATHON

Every spring astronomers gather to pay homage to Charles Messier, a French comet hunter who lived in the eighteenth century. Because his telescopes were small and inefficient by modern standards all the objects he found are the best and brightest galaxies, clusters, and nebulae in the northern sky. Messier published a list of over one hundred objects during his life. More were added from searching his papers after his death.

The Messier Marathon is an attempt to see them all, 110 of them, in one night's observing. Many people accept this challenge to see them all in one dusk-to-dawn session.

One of the best-attended Messier Marathons is in Arizona. The coordinator for many years of this event has been my friend AJ Crayon. He has done a wonderful job getting the word out for people to show up and enjoy the All-Arizona Messier Marathon at a location between Phoenix and Tucson. There have been folks gathered there in the hundreds trying to view the Messier objects as they pass overhead and near the horizons, east and west.

One of the fascinating things about this site is the street names as you drive to the location at the Farnsworth Ranch. Someone obviously knew quite a bit about astronomy and decided to use constellation names for the streets.

Me at the corner of Sagittarius and Gemini

Early in the evening there are lots of galaxies to find and then get the clusters in Cassiopeia, Perseus, and Auriga. Don't forget the Orion Nebula—who could do such a thing? Now on to lots of spring galaxies in Leo, Virgo, Coma Berenices, and Ursa Major. If you are ahead of the rising sky enough you can get a two-hour nap and wake up to the summer Milky Way. There is lots of do in Sagittarius, Scorpius, and Ophiuchus. Then get the late risers and you are done.

It is fun to spend a whole night watching the movement of the sky. There is rotation around the Pole and the obvious movement east to west across the middle of the sky.

Lots of fun people show up at the All-Arizona Messier Marathon, including Paul Lind and a fourteen-inch Newtonian he built.

Tom Polakis and his twenty-inch Dobsonian ready to soak up light from the Messier objects

Matt Luttinen and his twelve-inch on a mount he constructed

Joe Goss setting up his fourteen-inch Celestron Schmidt Cassegrain Telescope

Before the Sun goes down there is a meeting of the participants so that they can be clear about the rules. Actually, the rules are quite simple, just find all the Messier objects you can and check them off the list as you observe them. Then return the list to AJ or one of his helpers before you leave in the morning.

A meeting of the participants before the marathon begins

I have a distinction that I am proud of in relation to the Messier Marathon. AJ provides a certificate of participation for everyone who finds at least fifty Messier objects on the evening of the marathon. I received one of these certificates for finding eighty objects during the 2002 marathon; it is on the wall facing me right now. I am still to this day the recipient of an award for the smallest aperture. I used my 8X42 binoculars.

Me with the binoculars I used in finding eighty objects during a Messier Marathon

The little 8X42s are great for wide-field views of the Milky Way. The dark lanes that cut through our galaxy are fascinating from a dark site in these binoculars. Large open clusters are also fascinating. Viewing the Belt of Orion or the Double Cluster with these binoculars is mesmerizing. There is so much to see: chains of stars, star colors, and small grouping that just cannot be seen with the naked eye.

I also have a pair of 10X50 binoculars. Remember that the first number is the magnification and the second is the size of the objective in millimeters. So these binoculars magnify ten times and have 50mm (two-inch) lenses for each eye. The higher magnification provides the ability to see more individual stars within a cluster or along the Milky Way, and the larger lenses shows fainter stars and nebulosity. But these bigger binoculars have a smaller field of view. There is always a tradeoff.

My point is that there is plenty to see in a good pair of binoculars and they are easy to use and have an almost instantaneous set-up time. I like to sit in a chair, so the folding chair needs to be set up also. Like that is a problem. I hope I have convinced you to consider binoculars for astronomy; it is worth the time, money, and effort.

CHAPTER 19: SEPTEMBER 27, 2003

◯ꞟ◯

FIRST FIVE-MILE MEADOW TRIP

Part of the adventure of enjoying the night sky is searching for observing sites. We have had lots of fun driving around searching out new spots where we can set up the telescopes and have fun viewing. One of the limitations is that if we are looking for a site where the club can set up we will need lots of room. The good news about the Saguaro Astronomy Club is that if you create a great place to use for a star party, they will show up in droves.

The bad news about living in Phoenix, Arizona, is that it is hot. Often a summer day will reach 115 degrees Fahrenheit and continue at that daytime temperature for a month. So the need to get out of the hot valley around Phoenix and get up into the cool pine tree country in the northern part of Arizona becomes overwhelming.

We found a spot about forty miles east of Flagstaff that consists of a huge meadow that can accommodate lots of observers. It turns out that this location is about four miles from the site of the new Discovery Channel telescope. We did not plan it that way, but it was nice to see that professional astronomers came to the same location as our astronomy club.

After a chat with the ranger who manages this part of the forest, we got clear on the rules. No parking in the center of the meadow and no open fires except in the fire pits. We also agreed to furnish a portable toilet to keep the forest as pristine as possible.

We called the place "Five-Mile Meadow," because it is five miles along a dirt road after you turn off the paved road—simple enough. We picked a New Moon weekend and told the club members to be prepared for cold temperatures and gave out directions in the newsletter. By Saturday night there were thirty-two vehicles and telescopes all set up and ready to view a clear night sky.

Five-Mile Meadow filled with telescopes and ready for a great night of observing

Once it got dark we realized what a great place this was for observing the night sky. We were over one hundred miles from the lights of Phoenix, and it was dark. The altitude was about 6,900 feet, so the stars twinkled very little. I rated the seeing at eight out of ten and the transparency at nine out of ten, a terrific night.

In this photo with a 35mm lens at f/4 in a two-minute exposure, the dark rift in the Milky Way is obvious as it cuts through the constellation of Cygnus the Swan. Notice the stars well below the tree line. I also caught a meteor in the upper right of this photo.

I decided to use a 100mm (four-inch) refractor for the weekend. It has a focal ratio of f/6; this means that it is six times longer than the aperture of four inches. This also means that it is an RFT, a rich-field telescope. An RFT will provide wide fields of view to capture lots of sky in a low-power eyepiece and is great for viewing along the Milky Way.

Me with the four-inch RFT refractor and Five-Mile Meadow in the background

IC 4665 in Ophiuchus is a very large open cluster. Using my 8X42 binoculars I could resolve eleven stars in a ring shape. It was bright, very large, and not compressed toward the center. With the four-inch f/6 telescope and a 27mm eyepiece, I could resolve twenty-two stars in a ring layout that was immediately obvious. This cluster was bright, very large, and not compressed, and there were few faint members.

An image of IC 4665 with a 300mm lens and a four-minute exposure with a Canon Xt camera

The Dark Horse in Ophiuchus has been discussed before, but it was so prominent on this night that I need to give some observations from the Five-Mile Meadow site. On this night the Dark Horse figure was easily seen with the naked eye. I pointed it out to several others at the site. Using the four-inch f/6 with a 22mm eyepiece provided a great view; there was lots of contrast between the dark markings and the starry background. I could easily see the stars that outlined the Stem of the Pipe and the dark lanes that extended north and more prominently to the south of the "Stem" feature. The bowl of the Pipe Nebula is designated Barnard 59.

Barnard 63 is the prancing front leg of the horse; this extended dark marking was easy to see with the four-inch scope and the 22mm eyepiece. This entire area shows a fascinating interplay of darkness and contrast.

This photo with a 35mm lens and Fuji 800 film shows Antares as the bright star in the middle right and the Dark Horse on his hind leg, which is the Pipe Nebula.

M 24 is also called the Small Sagittarius Star Cloud. It is an extremely dense area of stars that is above the spout of the "Teapot" asterism. This elongated bright area in the Milky Way is easily visible with the naked eye on a transparent night. There are two dark nebulae on the north side of M 24; they are B 92 and B 93.

On this excellent night at Five-Mile Meadow, M 24 was absolutely fascinating. By the naked eye it was obvious, elongated east-west 2.5X1, and somewhat brighter in the middle. I could see that the oval was wider on the west side. Averted vision made it grow in size. Using the 10X50 binoculars I could count forty-six stars resolved, and there were several nice chains of stars involved. The dark nebulae were obvious on the north side of the star cloud. This silvery, elongated star grouping was lovely. Several dark lanes in the Milky Way were nearby.

This very large star cloud really shows off in the RFT refractor. With a 27mm eyepiece there are sixty-eight stars counted and a sparkling background that included several nice curved chains of stars. The star cloud was very bright and extremely large, elongated 2X1, and a little brighter in the middle. A prominent dark lane on the south side cut off the star cloud and made it really stand out. The two dark ovals were easy to see. This part of the sky has been a favorite of mine since the first time I went through the Messier objects.

A four-minute exposure using the Canon Xt of the area around the Small Sagittarius Star Cloud, M 24

NGC 7000 is the North America Nebula. This large area of nebulosity needs an RFT to be seen in its entirety. A dim glow can be seen in the area with the naked eye, and 10X50 binoculars will show the North America shape.

The North America shape really stood out with the four-inch RFT, a 35mm wide-field eyepiece, and a two-inch UHC filter. This setup provided a "wow" view of this famous object. It was bright, very, very large, and very irregular figure (North America) and showed forty-one stars involved. The dark lane on the east side that cuts off the nebula was very prominent and had an orange star involved. The section that is "Mexico" was the brightest; it had high surface brightness. The Pelican nebula was easily seen at the edge of the field. The star density on the north side of the nebula was amazing, with lots of faint and very faint stars. It was more obvious with the filter removed and the 22mm eyepiece and no filter. Without the filter the nebula was much fainter, but the starry glow was fascinating from this dark site.

The North America Nebula using a seven-minute exposure with a 135mm lens and my Canon Xt digital SLR. The camera has the Hutech modification so that the nebula shows up with more contrast.

I think that every time I am under truly dark skies and the summer Milky Way is up, I spend at least a few minutes with the area around the star Antares. This red giant is the heart of Scorpius.

With the RFT refractor this part of the sky is absolutely captivating. The 27mm eyepiece will allow you to see Antares as a bright orange star, and M 4 is a fascinating globular cluster nearby. At high power I can resolve twelve stars in M 4. There is a bright bar feature across the cluster, and extending out from the bar are several curved chains of stars that give it a ragged appearance.

NGC 6144 is a very compact globular cluster that is closer to Antares than M 4. I cannot resolve it into stars, but it does have a bright core. Beside some bright nebulae, there are two prominent dark lanes that exit the field to the northeast. All in all, this is a captivating area of the sky, and any star chart or planetarium program will keep you busy around here for many hours.

My image of the area around Antares. It was taken with an 85mm lens and a two-minute exposure using the Canon Xt with the Hutech modification.

It is a sad duty of mine to report within this book the fact that David Fredericksen died as I was writing it. David's passing is one of the great sorrows of my life. We spent many hours together under dark Arizona skies. He and I look somewhat alike, and many people thought we were brothers. It always brought me joy to think that someone would believe that David and I were brothers. In actuality we were both only children. I will miss my friend.

David viewing sunspots

One of my favorite stories about David involves me looking over his shoulder while he was drawing some really small cluster of stars, maybe a dozen members or so. I said, "David, why are you drawing that thing?"

He replied, "So I will never look again."

As a tribute to David, the members of the Saguaro Astronomy Club have decided to call this observing location "Fredericksen Meadow." I have no doubt that David is smiling about that choice. I hope to feel his presence each time I have a chance to return to this dark-sky site.

The Milky Way over Fredericksen Meadow

Chapter 20: April 1, 2005

The Second Australia Trip

I was in the middle of writing a book on nebulae and it occurred to me that lots of great nebulae can only be seen from the southern hemisphere. With that in mind I arranged for a flight to Australia and made an observing list for some goodies that I could only see after a fourteen-hour plane flight. I packed my list, the pair of 8X42 binoculars, and some eyepieces and was ready to see southern skies again.

Jim and Lynn Barclay were pleased to hear that I was coming down for a visit and set me up with a room and telescopes in the backyard. And ... I can write it off on my taxes. Please don't tell the IRS I said that. What more can one observer ask for?

After living too close to the growing city of Brisbane and its light pollution, the Barclays decided to move out into the country. They found a pretty large piece of land about sixty miles northeast of Brisbane and built a house and a backyard that contains five telescopes. This is my kind of backyard.

Jim and Lynn Barclay's backyard, with lots of telescopes and some pretty dark skies in which to use them

Jim Barclay with one of the Celestron fourteen-inch Schmidt-Cassegrain Telescopes (SCT) in his backyard. Being able to show up at his observing site and have telescopes already balanced and align to the south celestial Pole made the taking of astrophotos much easier.

I decided to start out simple, and for the first night I did some naked-eye observing and used the 8X42 binoculars for a few hours until the Moon rose at about 11:30. Eta Carina was obvious to the naked eye, and the Coal Sack was an easily seen dark oval. The second brightest star, Canopus, was up about twenty-five degrees, and Sirius was obviously brighter than Canopus.

Orion was lying on its side near the western horizon and was setting with the nebula *up* … very strange.

Alpha and Beta Centauri are two bright stars within the Milky Way, and they pointed to the Southern Cross. This entire region of the sky stood out very well. The False Cross in Vela was larger than the real Cross (Crux); but Crux had brighter stars and had Alpha and Beta Centauri pointing at it!

A wide-angle photo of the southern Milky Way. Alpha and Beta Centauri are to the left and point toward the dark oval Coal Sack. The Coal Sack is near the Southern Cross, four stars to its right. The brightest part of this image is Eta Carina, near the center. All these astrophotos were shot by Jim Barclay and myself on Fuji 400 film. This is an eight-minute exposure with a 28mm lens.

The Large Magellanic Cloud (LMC) was the bright cloud that doesn't move! The Tarantula Nebula was a bright spot on one end of the LMC. The Large and Small Magellanic Clouds are satellite galaxies of the Milky Way. They are far enough south that Europeans had never seen them. They only found out about the clouds when the first circumnavigation of the globe was completed by the sailors of Magellan and they returned with stories of these bright clouds that circle the southern pole.

Picking up the 8X42 binoculars, the LMC showed as a giant L-shaped glow with the bright Tarantula Nebula at the short end of the "L." This relatively nearby galaxy was extremely bright, extremely large, and very little brighter in the middle, and it appeared to take up about half of the binocular field of view.

An image of the LMC taken with a 300mm lens

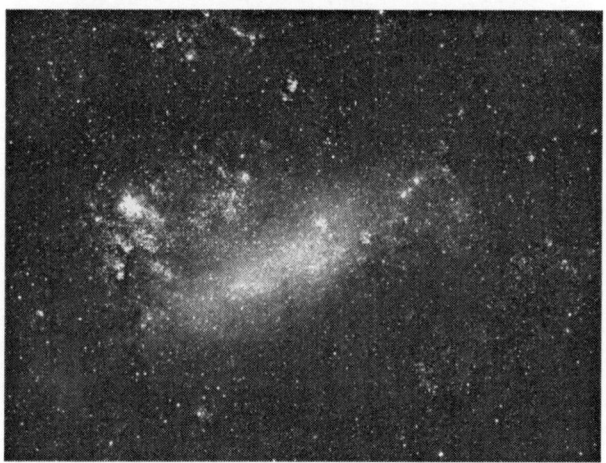

The Eta Carina Nebula is about twice the size of the Orion Nebula and is brighter because of sixteen stars involved. Eta Carinae itself is the brightest star within the nebula and is obviously light orange in binoculars! I saw an obvious dark lane cutting the nebula into one-third, two-thirds portions. The star cloud in which Eta Carina is embedded was *rich*—an amazing profusion of faint and very faint stars in the 8X42s. The cloud was elongated 5X1 and cut off top and bottom by dark lanes that were easy in the little binoculars. It was much like the Cygnus Star Cloud.

NGC 3532 is a very rich and bright-open cluster to the east of Eta Carina. This is a "wow" object in binoculars. There were twenty stars resolved with the binoculars. I saw it as very bright, very large, much compressed, and very rich. There was an obvious orange star to the left of this cluster and many dark lanes in this area.

Eta Carina with a 200mm lens; it is an eight-minute exposure on Fuji 400 film. The cluster on the left is NGC 3532.

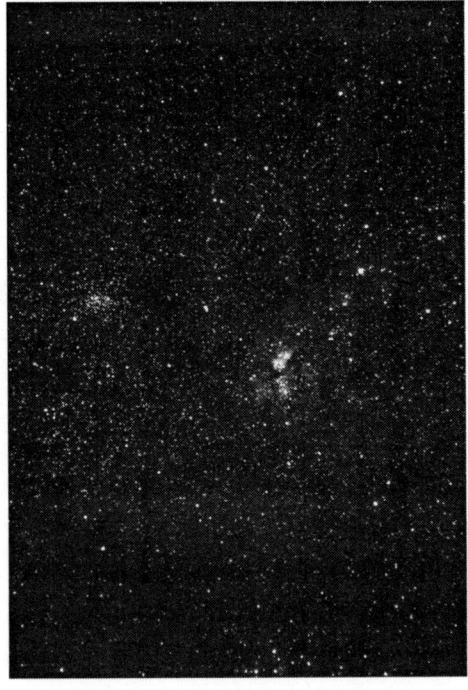

In the binoculars the Coal Sack showed as a dark elongated cloud with twenty stars involved. It was not one solid dark area; there were striations of light and dark within the Coal Sack. It had a small elongated dark section right at the edge of the Milky Way.

The Dark Doodad was a long dark lane within the constellation of Musca, the Fly. It was easily seen with the binoculars, and the western side was longer and easier to see. There were globular clusters at both ends of the dark curved dark lane.

The Dark Doodad begins on the right center of this photo and is less obvious when it gets to the middle of the shot.

Because the skies were so dark and the dark lanes within the Milky Way so easily seen when the sky is dark, ancient tribes created dark constellations. In South America and Australia these ancient peoples made mythological happenings in the sky include dark creatures as well as the usual "connect the dots" constellations we are used to.

The largest and most prominent of these is the Dark Emu. This is an Australian bird, much like an ostrich, that meanders along over thirty degrees of the southern Milky Way. The Dark Emu is easy to recognize once seen, an unmistakable and huge dark bird that goes from the Coal Sack to Scorpius … one of the sky's most fascinating views with no optical aid. There is an eye within the Coal Sack, and the dark "beak" extends to the bottom of the Southern Cross; down the neck that includes A+B Centauri, the body thickens and the legs move off toward southern Scorpius, and the tail feathers above that toward the head of the Scorpion.

A photo with a 28mm lens showing the Dark Emu with its head at the top of the picture, which is the Coal Sack. Antares is at the bottom left, and the legs of the Emu are to the right of Antares.

All of the rest of these observations were made using the telescope set up under the dome in Jim Barclay's backyard. There was a five-inch f/8 refractor alongside a twelve-inch f/15 Cassegrain.

NGC 2070 is the Tarantula Nebula in the LMC. Using the five-inch with an 18mm eyepiece showed it as very bright, large, and having a bright middle. The spider shape of the Tarantula Nebula was obvious; averted vision filled in the legs of the spider shape. Moving up to the twelve-inch with a 40mm eyepiece provided a great view. The Tarantula shape was 60 percent of the FOV, with twenty-six stars involved. Nebulosity was in beautiful streamers out from the cluster at the center. Adding the two-inch UHC filter made it spectacular. The contrast between the dark lanes and the bright nebulosity was excellent.

A photo of NGC 2070 by Jim Barclay made with a C 14 using a telecompressor so that it shot the image at f/6

NGC 2477 is a rich open cluster in Puppis. In the five-inch with a 30mm eyepiece it showed bright, large, extremely rich, and extremely compressed. This cluster was very well detached from the Milky Way background. With an 18mm eyepiece there were seventeen stars counted in the northeast quadrant of this cluster; therefore the entire cluster showed at least sixty stars resolved. There was a beautiful chain of stars off to the north with two double stars in that chain, a great view of a great cluster. In the twelve-inch scope with the 40mm eyepiece there were eighty stars resolved in the northeast quadrant; so the entire cluster showed well over three hundred stars resolved. There were many pairs and chains of stars. This rich cluster took up 70 percent of the field and sparkled like gemstones. This cluster is a favorite and is truly magnificent when it is sixty degrees above the horizon!

NGC 3132 is one of the most beautiful planetary nebulae in the sky. In the five-inch with an 18mm eyepiece there was an obvious nebulous disk that was elongated and showed a central star. Averted vision made it larger. Using the twelve-inch scope with a 30mm eyepiece provided a great view. This planetary showed bright, pretty large, and elongated 1.5X1 in a PA of 135 degrees. The central star was obvious, and the disk showed a light-green color. There was a hint of annular structure with "fill in" nebulosity. Raising the magnification with an 18mm eyepiece made the annular structure more obvious. Averted vision showed a very faint outer glow around the bright inner section.

A photo of NGC 3132 made by Jim Barclay
with the twelve-inch telescope

NGC 3372 is the Eta Carina nebula. It is one of the reasons that riding on an airliner for fourteen hours is worth it. Using the five-inch with a 30mm eyepiece showed this to be like no other place in the sky. There was nebulosity within this entire field of view. It faded out to the south into a very rich field of stars. Even with the small scope there were about one hundred stars involved, including delicate pairs and chains throughout. Dark markings cut the nebula into one-third, two-third sections, and there were several "elephant trunks" of dark nebulosity. Lowering the power with a two-inch 40mm eyepiece and using the UHC filter provided an amazing view. The nebulosity was framed perfectly. There were loops of light and dark nebulosity intertwined in a very rich star field. In the twelve-inch scope with a 30mm eyepiece and no filter, the Humoculous was an obvious light-orange color; this central section contained the star Eta Carina within an elongated shell. I saw this shell as elongated 1.5X1 around Eta Carina, and it included a delicate web of dark markings on the glowing figure-eight nebulosity. There was a delicate triple star just to the north about one arc minute.

Eta Carina captured by Jim Barclay with his twelve-inch Newtonian

NGC 3532 is one of the richest open star clusters in the sky. Viewing with the five-inch and a 30mm eyepiece, I could resolve seventy-seven stars. The cluster was very bright, large, and elongated 2X1. The brightest member was sunshine yellow. There was a dark lane down the middle. In the twelve-inch with a 40mm eyepiece, this cluster was 100 percent of the field of view. There were several delicate pairs within the cluster. It appeared to be completely resolved with this scope and magnification; there were very few faint and very faint members. With the larger scope there were over two hundred members resolved.

Alpha Centauri is one of the most amazing double stars in the sky. In the twelve-inch telescope with 40mm eyepiece it was an easy split. What is unique about this double star is that it is composed of a first-magnitude and a second-magnitude pair of stars. No other place in the sky provides two stars this bright so close together. This double star is unique and beautiful. The three-vane spider gives a great pattern of color and sparkles as their patterns overlap.

NGC 5139—you didn't think I was going to travel all the way to Australia and then not talk about Omega Centauri! From Jim's observatory this amazing cluster was seventy degrees above the horizon! From one of my favorite observing sites in Arizona it gets only eleven degrees above the horizon. From Australia, I found it by going "up" from Beta Centauri. In the twelve-inch scope and a 40mm eyepiece Omega Centauri was 90 percent of the field of view, an amazing globe of stars. I counted 105 stars in the northeast quadrant, so the total number of stars was over four hundred. This huge cluster had a pretty smooth stellar distribution, except for a prominent chevron of about eight stars on the southeast edge. There is a fascinating effect with the twelve-incher; as I use direct vision on one section of the cluster, I automatically used averted vision on another section, so the number of resolved stars flashed on and off as I looked around this stunning ball of stars.

Omega Centauri from Jim Barclay with the twelve-inch Newtonian

When the observing was over I took Flight 175 directly from Brisbane to LA. Southern skies were gone for a while. The part of the sky that was "missing" from Arizona was stunning. The Magellanic Clouds, the Milky Way from Vela to Norma, and its stunning variety of clusters, nebulae, and beautiful star fields were all worth the trip. I was *so* glad that I brought the binoculars; the ability to compare the viewing with the same instrument on both north and south skies was invaluable. There were several good movies to pass the time while flying home. I think I will try *The Incredibles*.

Chapter 21: 2010

⁓⁂⁓

My Telescopes
through the Years

After having a chance to own a variety of telescopes over the years, I have learned much about telescopes in general and the ones I possessed in particular. It might be helpful to share that knowledge with you now. This will be a chronological listing of each scope and some information about it.

I saw one thing right away, and that was that a set-up or teardown time of around half an hour was imperative. If a telescope took far more than that, it was just too clumsy to use and I would start making excuses so that this scope would not get used. The convenient telescope goes out observing the sky; the difficult-to-use telescope stays home.

The first telescope I bought was an eight-inch f/6 Meade Newtonian, model 856. For what I paid in 1978, it was a good telescope. I saw lots of the sky with it, and before I succumbed to aperture fever it proved to be an excellent starter scope. It had enough aperture to show plenty of detail on bright objects and was small enough to be easily set up and ready to go.

I also learned that I was not going to be an astrophotographer. I wanted to be one, but I found that I really enjoyed viewing the sky more than trying to take photos. My first night of photography I hit

205

the declination shaft with my knee and turned the entire scope over on its back. Trying to do complex activities in the dark is not easy.

My college roommate, Frank Zullo, setting up the scope in our backyard near Arizona State University

After a night of observing the sky near Saguaro Lake here I am viewing the distant Four Peaks mountains.

I have already admitted to getting aperture fever, so I started thinking about a larger telescope than the eight-inch. I sold off that telescope and ordered the 17.5-inch mirror from Coulter Optical. I have already discussed the construction of this scope in the second chapter. My ambitions about photographing the sky had now completely gone away; an Alt-Az telescope that is moved by hand will not track the sky to allow photos.

I enjoyed this telescope, it was not the best mirror, but it was good enough for me to see detail in a variety of deep-sky objects. Any Messier globular cluster was fabulous in the telescope at 200X. Dark lanes and bright spots in the arms of galaxies could be viewed from a good observing site.

It has been thirty years since I owned my 17.5-inch, and even today telescopes in the range of sixteen to eighteen inches are still very popular. Virtually all the manufacturers of commercial telescopes make an instrument in that size range. The reason is that they will show an observer much more than an eight- or ten-inch telescope, and yet they are much easier to get ready than a twenty-four-inch or larger.

The 17.5 in f/4.5 Dobsonian and me, also near Four Peaks

After owning the 17.5-inch scope for several years, I wanted to see what a telescope of that size with a more accurately made mirror would do. So I built the largest telescope I ever owned, an eighteen-inch f/6 Dobsonian. The mirror was ground and polished by John Hall of Pegasus Optics, and it was excellent. The views were spectacular; this telescope really worked well at 300X, something the 17.5-inch never did. Even at lower magnifications, this scope provided a sharp view with very good contrast.

But this telescope did not meet the criteria I set forth in the beginning of this chapter. It took forty-five minutes of hot, sweaty work to get set up and ready to use. I was okay with that for a while, but it got tiresome as time went on.

Even though the views were excellent, the effort to use this telescope was wearing, and I was ready to move on when my Australian buddy offered me a reasonable price to buy the mirror and take it back to Australia. I said yes to the deal, and the mirror of the eighteen-incher was on its way south. The Brisbane Astronomical Society built an observatory for this scope, which is exactly what it needed.

The eighteen-inch at Sentinel, Arizona

I had become attracted to drawing what I saw at the eyepiece. When using a Dobsonian, you must pull the scope along as the object moves through the field. This adds a layer of complication to making a good drawing. I had decided that my next telescope would have a driven mount, like the Meade eight-incher. A driven mount will use a battery-operated motor and gear mechanism to move the scope at the rate the stars move overhead. This means that whatever you are viewing will stay in the field of view of the eyepiece as you observe. I was drawing many objects that I viewed in the telescope, and having a driven mount would make it much easier.

Another shot of the eighteen-inch telescope, with Curt Taylor (left) and me for scale

I knew that driven telescopes in the same size as the eighteen-inch were beyond my budget, so I looked for something a little smaller with a driven mount. The universe supplied me with Pierre Schwaar. He had been making telescopes in the Tucson area and had recently moved to Phoenix. Pierre and I agreed on a price, and he started grinding me a thirteen-inch f/5.6 Newtonian mirror; this tube assembly would fit on one of Pierre's Bigfoot mounts. This was an invention of Pierre's, a wooden German Equatorial mount that is large enough to handle scope such as the thirteen-inch.

I had him grind the mirror to f/5.6 so that the tube assembly fit into my long-bed Toyota truck. You have to answer the question

"How will I move this thing around?" before you buy the telescope. Otherwise you will find yourself going shopping for a vehicle after you have purchased your "telescope of a lifetime."

This is the telescope I used for fourteen years, and I only moved on because I had observed all that I wanted to see with that telescope. There are several SAC members who still own and use their Bigfoot telescopes. I sold mine to a friend who teaches high school near Prescott. He has trained the students to use it, and they are still viewing the sky with it to this day.

Thirteen-inch in f/5.6 Newtonian, mirror, and Bigfoot mount from the late Pierre Schwaar (left). I used it for fourteen years and viewed the northern sky contents of Burnham's Celestial Handbook *with this scope.*

Me and the thirteen-inch Newtonian, easily the telescope I owned for the longest time

I have always enjoyed a wide-field view of the sky, and I decided to try a smaller scope that gave a wide view. Bill Anderson had a six-inch f/6 that he was not using because he had an eight-inch that he liked more. Bill had rigged it up with setting circles so that you could use it with a calculator to determine exactly where to point the scope and get the object you were looking for into the field of view. I know that there are many thousands of such scopes today, but in 1995 it was a novel idea.

This telescope provided good views of the sky and gave a good, but not great, field of view. I used it for several years and enjoyed the time I had with it, but I found that I wanted more. Do notice the huge 38mm Giant Erfle eyepiece on this scope. This eyepiece is World War II surplus; it was used in the periscope of a Sherman tank. In an era before the huge, heavy eyepieces we have today, it was a good wide-field eyepiece.

The six-inch f/6 Newtonian and me with a T-shirt showing William Herschel, my hero

In the time from 1999 until now, I did a lot of buying and selling of telescopes. I did not set out to do so; it just turned out that way.

My next purchase was a six-inch f/6 Maksutov-Newtonian from Orion. It was a terrific wide-field telescope and worked great at high magnification also. The images were excellent, with tiny star points and much detail at higher powers.

I liked the scope, and it was well mounted on a Losmandy German equatorial mount. The combination of a large, well-made mount and a rather small telescope certainly created a solidly mounted instrument. I used it with a set of electronic setting circles, and I found that I really liked being able to point the telescope accurately at any of the large number of deep-sky objects in the memory.

This is the only scope I have owned in all these years that I can say I regret selling off. But I may replace it one of these days.

The six-inch in f/6 Maksutov-Newtonian on Losmandy G-11 mount at Sentinel

Then I went to Riverside in 2001 and fell in love. The latest Nexstar 11 GPS was being displayed, and David and I both really liked what we saw. It is an eleven-inch Schmidt-Cassegrain telescope that provided excellent contrast and a pretty sharp field of view. I really liked the electronics. In the past much of our time under dark skies was spent trying to find the object you were searching to see. The Nexstar system made that all a thing of the past. Once you aligned the mount to two stars very accurately it just found things all night long. Amazing!

I purchased my Nexstar 11 GPS from Starizona in Tucson. I owned that scope for six years, it was a very trustworthy scope, and I saw a lot with it. I simply got the itch to try something new and different.

The Nexstar 11 GPS with a four-inch refractor piggybacked

Meanwhile, in the observatory in Phoenix, I decided I had enough of trying to repair the Meade seven-inch Maksutov. The electronics were a constant source of aggravation, and I wanted to replace this telescope. So I sold the seven-inch Mak and bought an eight-inch Celstron Nexstar to put into the observatory. This made a big difference it two ways.

First, now I had a system that really could find things accurately from the backyard. I started searching out double stars with this scope and had a great time for years looking at multiple stars. Once I got it all set up, it never missed.

Second, the hand paddle of the scope I took out to dark skies (the Nexstar 11 GPS) and the hand paddle of the scope in the observatory were identical. So I did not have to remember which scope was which, and it saved me a lot of grief and mental gymnastics.

In the observatory the Nexstar 8 GPS takes over from the Meade Maksutov

02/06/2006

Once I sold off the Nexstar 11 I got hooked on refractors, and I have had one ever since. My first refractor was another scope that was aimed at getting wide fields of view. It was a four-inch f/6 Orion refractor. I used it on an Orion Sirius mount. This setup worked quite well. The mount was beefy enough to hold the little refractor in a steady manner.

This small refractor had the usual trouble with inexpensive refractors—color. If you aimed it a bright star like Vega and put in a high-power eyepiece it was psychedelic; lots of blue and purple swirls of color that turned on and off with the seeing. So don't do that! It is not what this telescope was made to accomplish.

If, however, you aim this telescope at any Messier open cluster or the Double Cluster or the Orion Nebula or along the Summer Milky Way, you are in for a treat. There is good contrast between the stars and dark lanes. Bright nebulae are surrounded by a sea of stars that can't be seen with a high power, narrow field telescope. No one telescope can do it all.

The Orion four-inch refractor on the Sirius mount at the Five-Mile Meadow site near Happy Jack. What a great night for looking up and down the Milky Way.

Now that I am firmly hooked by refractors, I decided to try a larger one ... could you see that coming? I found a deal on the Cloudy Nights website and sent off the money order to get it delivered. Once the scope showed up, I got it all mounted on the Sirius mount. Then I had it made clear to me that this was just not enough mount for the six-inch f/8 Celestron refractor. When I touched the focuser to get a sharper focal point the scope wiggled for ten seconds. Rather exasperating, wouldn't you say?

The six-inch f/8 Celestron refractor on Orion Sirius mount

08/10/2007

I started looking for a new mount, and the folks at Starizona in Tucson came through again. I decided to try the new Celestron CGEM and am very happy with its performance. Now the big refractor is well mounted and the commands are very similar to the old Nexstar system, so there is little "retraining" to be done.

This setup is so good that I created an observing list around this particular scope and mount. I called it the "Small Telescope Project." I added together the Messier objects, the brightest NGC, the best multiple stars, and some asterisms that are favorites of mine. All this available on the Saguaro Astronomy Club website (www. saguaroastro.org).

Me with the six-inch refractor on the CGEM mount at the Oregon Star Party in 2009. Lots of fun.

Once I finished observing the objects in the "Small Telescope Project" I got the itch to try astrophotography again. The CGEM mount lends itself to doing this, and so I kept it and sold off the big refractor and some other accessories to acquire a wide-field photographic rig. I settled on an ED 80mm guiding for a William Optics Megrez 110mm. I had been using a Canon 350D camera with the Hutech modification for some time to take images through simple DSLR camera lenses.

At the Table Mountain Star Party in the state of Washington I had nothing but trouble. At one point I had about five people surrounding me trying to help. I wasted eight hours of clear skies and never got the imaging system up and working. I am sorry; I have little patience for this type of stuff, so I gave up. I sold off both refractors at the star party and hope that the people who purchased them are having a great time and are getting good results.

Astronomy Magazine will just have to deal with not having my images for the cover next month.

Table Mountain Star Party

It seems to me that once one door closes, another opens. The folks at the Sun River Observatory in Oregon were selling a Televue TV 102 refractor. It has an aperture of 102mm (four inches) and a focal ratio around f/8. The views with it are excellent. Sharp star images are seen with this excellent refractor, easily the best views of the sky I have had with a small telescope. Viewing along the Milky Way with the 27mm Panoptic eyepiece is a real joy with this telescope.

The TV 102 on the CGEM mount set up at the Antennas Site, far from the lights of Phoenix

You know me by now; I always want some more aperture. Again, a member of the Cloudy Nights gang puts just what I want up for sale. I buy a 9.25-inch Celestron SCT in excellent condition. These tube assemblies are famous for sharp views with great contrast, and mine is no different.

I split a double that had a separation of 1.4 arc seconds and was able to show it to Dick Harshaw. He is the president of SAC and has much experience with viewing double stars. When he says a scope is a good performer, I believe him. I know that for a few of you, a split of 1.4 arc seconds is a "ho hum" evening. In central Arizona that is a pretty rare night.

The 9.25 SCT on the CGEM mount, again at the Antennas Site

There are a variety of things that I have learned from owning all these telescopes. Here they are in no particular order:

There is no such thing as a good, cheap telescope. Many people buy an inexpensive department store telescope for Christmas or give it to a child for their birthday. Very often they are just a disappointment. A decent starter scope costs several hundred dollars whatever you do, and there is no getting around that. Join your local astronomy club or get on the Cloudy Nights website. There is a beginner's forum with questions from novices, and we will try to give you a good answer.

There is no such thing as an all-purpose telescope. No scope will provide excellent views at high magnifications and then drop down to also provide wide-field, high-contrast views of the Milky Way. If you invent one, patent it right away. It is the reason that I have wound up with several telescopes over the years: one for wide field; one for high power. The good news is that they both fit my CGEM mount.

For large apertures, the seeing is going to be the limiting factor on many nights. If this is a well-made telescope then the highest usable magnification will be limited by the air overhead long before the figure of the mirror or the brand of eyepiece you are using.

Which leads me to one of AJ's famous statements: "Eyepieces are a religious discussion." Assuming you have a good telescope, then the rest of the viewing is done by the combination of the eyepiece, the eye, and the brain. If you have some eyepieces that fit the way you like to observe, they are the "correct" eyepieces. There are several brands of expensive eyepieces that just don't fit my eye. Either I have to get so close to the glass that I feel cramped or I cannot find the right position for my head and eye to get the most out of the eyepiece. Many observers use and like these same eyepieces I can't or won't use. Try out an eyepiece before you buy it, or make certain that the company has a good return policy before reading out that credit card number. This is another place where joining an astronomy club makes a difference, you can try out an eyepiece before buying it.

I think the most important lesson is that the easy-to-use telescope is the one that will get used. I learned this with the big, heavy eighteen-incher. It just stopped being fun having to set up and tear down that big telescope. The views with it were certainly excellent, but eventually it had to go.

Once I saw what a joy it was to step out to the observatory, roll back the roof, put in an eyepiece, flip a switch, and start observing, I was hooked. I got a lot of observing done when I had the convenience of a backyard observatory available to me.

I know that I have owned a variety of scopes over the years. I have no doubt AJ chuckles about the whole thing when he sees me with a new telescope. He has owned only two telescopes in thirty years. Maybe he just found the right scope quicker than I did, or maybe I just like having a scope that is new to me. It has certainly been a learning experience.

CHAPTER 22

THE FIVE THINGS IT HAS TAKEN
ME THIRTY-THREE YEARS TO LEARN

My sixty-second birthday is coming up, and so I have spent over half my life in the pursuit of dark skies, clear nights, steady seeing, and good friends with whom to share the view. I am fortunate that I have been a member of the Saguaro Astronomy Club for most of the time I have been an amateur astronomer; the camaraderie, enthusiasm, and knowledgeable members have been a joy to know over the years.

With that as a background, I would like to share a countdown of five things that I have determined are important if you are planning to really enjoy this avocation and give yourself a chance to see the most of our universe.

1) Show others the sky. Folks, you might not believe this, but if you can find five constellations and explain the phases of the Moon, you are *way* ahead of the average person on the street. Most people know very little about what there is to observe in the sky. Even if you are a beginner, please set up your telescope and show someone who is curious what there is to see. I set up my scope on the sidewalk in front of my house every Halloween. There is always a line of children yearning for a chance to see that bright planet for themselves. There is no substitute for looking at the sky with your own eyes. Also, it

will help you get in touch with the first time *you* saw the rings of Saturn.

2) You can observe, even in the city—just do it. There are a wide variety of things about the sky to observe, anytime, anywhere. Even if it is partly cloudy, there are color effects from the Sun and Moon. Sundogs, the ring around the Moon, and, obviously, rainbows are fascinating. All you have to do is keep looking up. Even with no optical aid you can watch the Moon moving among the stars and changing shape from night to night.

3) Stop worrying about equipment. Spending your time looking at the advertisements for appealing new gear is great. But you can do a lot with minimum equipment. Every time I go out to observe I spend a little time just looking at the beauty of the night sky. Just sit in that folding chair and soak in the beauty of the Milky Way and star colors and maybe spot a meteor or two. This is lots of fun and demands no equipment. Even though I do have a great new go-to telescope, I love to just pick up the 8X42 binoculars and scan the star clouds in the Milky Way and bright clusters and nebulae. You just don't need thousands of dollars of stuff to enjoy the beauty of the sky overhead. Okay, okay, this is from the guy who owned all the telescopes in Chapter 21; I get it.

4) Make a list of what you want to observe, tonight and far into the future. I have seen so much because I knew where I was going. It is certainly fun to just put in a wide-field eyepiece and scan the sky for whatever you bump into. However, most observers quickly want to know "what is the name of that cluster?" To make the most of that precious time under the stars, create a list of what you want to see tonight. Take some notes about what you saw and you will have a permanent record of that observation. I also like having a

long-term goal. There are plenty of lists on the SAC website (www.
saguaroastro.org). Another friend of mine, Tom Polakis, has been
writing a deep-sky observing column for *Astronomy Magazine* for
many years. Maybe your long-term project could be to see those
objects in your telescope.

5) Get with some other observers and share the fun. Regardless
of how you go about it, spending time under the stars is just more
fun if you share the joy. It is very gratifying to be able to show an
observing buddy something they have never seen before. It is also
great when you get to see a new cluster, galaxy, or nebula in the
telescope of a friend. The good news is that there are lots of ways to
get in touch with other astronomers. I have already mentioned one
of the most satisfying in my opinion, and that is a nearby astronomy
club. Most large cities have a club in their area. Call a librarian or the
planetarium. If you are an Internet user, the possibilities are massive.
Newsgroups, mailing lists, Yahoo groups, and many other outlets
provide an electronic astronomy club that meets twenty-four hours
a day. I spend much of my time online at the Cloudy Nights (www.
cloudynights.com) website.

The joy of viewing the universe in all its diversity will change your
life. There is something available to those of us who know the night
sky like a friend. You can look up, see a familiar constellation,
and know what season it is and why that season is now. Seeing a
"shooting star" takes on a new meaning when you know that tiny
meteoroid came from far away, at the edge of the solar system.

You can see a variable star and know that it is changing its size as it
changes its brightness. You can view a red carbon star and know that
a haze of dust blocks off the blue light from that star and makes it
appear red. A tiny speck of light in your telescope is a very distant

galaxy, a city of stars and nebulae so far away that it can barely be seen. How few people have ever observed those distant galaxies?

Seeing the grandeur and scale of the universe we live in will certainly give you a feel for how tiny the Earth and its inhabitants are. It will also give you a sense of wonder that we "figured it out." The amazing science of astronomy can provide you with knowledge about the size and age of the universe.

Even though our bodies are tiny specks in relation to the universe on any scale, we have powerful enough minds that can start down the path of understanding where we are within the universe and what the overall starscape looks like. That is quite amazing to me.

So here we are at the end of my third book. It has been fun writing up all these observing sessions, what we saw and how we got there. I hope that it encourages you to start your own journey along this path. It has brought joy to my life, and I wouldn't have missed a minute of it.

Clear skies to us all …

Steve Coe

E-mail: stevecoe@cloudynights.com

INDEX

Lightning Source UK Ltd.
Milton Keynes UK
UKOW04f0946020714

234423UK00001B/53/P